MW01633703

Amen

Speaking in Church with Purpose & Peace

Amen

Speaking in Church with Purpose & Peace

PERIHELION PRESS

PROVO, UTAH

Published by Perihelion Press
3214 N. University Ave. #404, Provo UT 84604
www.perihelionpress.com

Cover design by Barry Hansen
Interior design by Marny K. Parkin

Witt, Celeste Elain
Amen : speaking in Church with purpose and peace

ISBN 978-1-933434-01-8

Printed in the United States
10 9 8 7 6 5 4 3 2 1

Contents

Preface 11

Introduction: A Long Journey to the Pulpit 13

How to Use This Book 16

Realize Your Role in God's Kingdom 19

A Resounding Amen 20
What Makes a Good Sermon? 23
Let Your Light Shine 25
Respond with Gladness 27
Lifelong Preparation 29
Finding the Answers 31
A Blessing in the Burden 33
Teach Truth 35
Build Testmonies 37
Build Relationships 39
Build the Kingdom 40

Prepare Your Heart and Mind 45

Seek the Spirit 46
Four Lessons from the Savior 49
Seven Questions 51
Seven More Questions 54
Make Haste 56

Cleanse Our Hearts 58
Christ-Centered Sermons 61
Fulfill Your Purpose 63
A Strong Foundation 66
The Three Components of a Sermon 68
Listen to Great Talks 70

Feed the Savior's Flock 73

Spiritual Nourishment 74
Difficult Topics 76
Love Your Listeners 79
A Sermon's Power 81
Communicate with Love 83
The Golden Rule 85
What If I'm Boring? 87
Praise Ward Members 89
We Are All Temporary 91
Time Is a Gift 93
Carve Out Time 96
Fear of Hypocrisy 98

Search for Sacred Ideas 101

Sources of Truth 120
The Dictionary Is Our Friend 106
Use Well-Known Literature 108
The Savior Used Scriptures 111
Avoid Rumors 113
Who Said It? 115
Mark the Scriptures 117
Great Thoughts 119
Read Widely 121
Record Your Insights 124
Start with Plenty 126

Keep a Journal 128
Good Examples 131

Create a Meaningful Message 133

You Are Naturally Creative 134
A Plain Path 138
Select Your Topic 140
Develop a Mission Statement 142
Define Your Message 144
Use Scriptures Accurately 146
Speak Plainly 149
Make Quotes Stand Out 151
Take Notes 154
Seeing Is Believing 156
Engage the Senses 158
Anchor Sermons in Christ 160
Create a Sense of Urgency 166
Become a Guide 164
Words Have Meaning 167
Choose the Best Words 169
Quote the Word of God 171
Use Scriptures Effectively 174
Say More about Less 176
Your Stories Are Valuable 178
Speaking in Parables 180
Effective Storytelling 183
Can Humor Fit In? 185
Stories Touch Hearts 187
Use Names Reverently 189

Organize Your Ideas 193

Organize Your Ideas 194
What Are the Questions? 197

In the Beginning 199
Connect through a Salutation 201
Keep the Connection 203
Attract Your Audience 205
Reveal Your Topic 218
Establish Credibility 210
Give Listeners a Road Map 212
Make It Hard to Get Lost 214
Rule of Three 217
Choose the Best Order 219
From Milk to Meat 221
Don't Wander Off Course 223
Steps to Conclude 225
Signal the End Is Near 227
Reinforce Your Message 229

Calm Your Spirit 233

A Testimony of the Task 234
Prayer Brings Peace 236
Eliminate Self-Doubts 238
Do Not Fear Man 240
Build Your Confidence 242
Believe You Can Speak 244
Dress for the Occasion 246
Don't Point Out Your Faults 249
Get a Good Night's Rest 251

Deliver with Power 255

Use Your Whole Body 256
Eye Contact 278
Managing the Microphone 260
Speak to Be Heard 263
Paint with Your Voice 265

Loud and Soft 267
Avoid Filler Words 269
Use Your Hands 271
Learn to Gesture 274
Your Body Matters 276
Abandon Nervous Habits 279
Speak with Enthusiasm 280
Develop a Friendly Style 282
Rehearse Your Message 284
Gospel Grown-Ups 287
Charge Up Your Battery 289
Full Text or Notes? 291
Make Your Notes Work for You 294
Eyes Are Upon You 297
Shrink to Fit 300
Make Connections 302

Amen 305

Listen with the Spirit 306
Your Personal Testimony 308
Reverence for the Savior's Name 310
Amen 312

Worksheet 315

Sacrament Meeting Sermon Preparation Outline 316

Preface

Jesus saith unto him, Feed my sheep.

John 21:17

It was at the Sea of Galilee, that the resurrected Savior showed Himself to seven of His Apostles. He startled them as He asked Peter, "Lovest thou me?" Their lives had exemplified love and devotion and now this question hinted that the Lord had some doubt. Peter replied, "Yea, Lord; thou knowest that I love thee." The Savior's reply was short and to the point. "Feed my lambs." Twice more the scene was repeated, with the response from the Savior, "Feed my sheep" (John 21:15–17).

When the Savior said, "Feed my sheep," He was using a metaphor. It was a simple metaphor drawn from the world around Him. He used ordinary items to symbolize something He wanted to teach or explain. After all, we are not sheep. Nor, technically, is He a shepherd. But the image is compelling and has survived two thousand years of retelling and reinterpreting.

The symbolism, in its simplicity, is comfortable and rich with meaning. It's easy to call up an image of sheep with the Good Shepherd; the scene has been painted a thousand times—on canvas and in our minds.

What is sometimes overlooked, however, is the word "feed." Feed? What is it the Lord expects of us? What is He asking us to do?

The Lord wants us to provide spiritual nourishment. We nourish one another with the "pleasing word of God." Daily in our homes. Weekly in our meetings. And as often as possible in our interactions with others.

That idea is the springboard message of this book—that we consider carefully every opportunity we have to build the kingdom of God through the words we speak. One of the most precious of those opportunities, of course, is speaking in sacrament meeting.

Think of it. After singing a hymn about the Savior, you review your life, scrutinize your behavior, recommit to your baptismal covenant, call upon the powerful cleansing of the Atonement, and partake of the sacrament. At that moment you are probably more prepared than at any other time in the week to receive inspired counsel. You are hungry. Deeply hungry.

You are hoping that the delicious word of God will be served up to you in heaping, scrumptious portions—garnished with the compelling testimony of someone who is earnestly striving upward along the path toward heaven—just like you. Without giving lengthy consideration, you silently pray that the words spoken will be organized and delivered in a way that will make the message clear and the source undeniably divine. But where do sacrament meeting sermons like that come from? From the depths of a prepared soul who senses your hunger.

That is why *Amen* was written. Since we serve each other in the Church by preaching from the pulpit from time to time, we need to make the most of those few marvelous moments. The ideas in this book are simply thoughts and suggestions which, when studied, considered and applied, may improve your effectiveness when you speak.

You are a shepherd-in-training. Each day you spend with the flock, you will become more aware of what they need and how your words can meet that need. There is a special peace in knowing you have followed the Savior's request to "Feed my sheep."

Introduction: A Long Journey to the Pulpit

Speak good words to them.

1 Kings 12:7

Speaking in sacrament meeting should be a blessing in your life. It should also be a blessing to those who hear you speak.

For many, the goal is simply to survive until the final "Amen." But what if the experience of speaking in Church could be more? A lot more.

This book is designed for everyone, including me. There are steps that need to be taken every time you approach the opportunity to speak in Church. You may be an experienced speaker or a complete novice, but the process is really about the same. And that's what this book is all about—steps you can take to speak more effectively and more confidently.

Knowing these steps makes it so I love to speak now. But it hasn't always been that way. One early opportunity to speak in Church was particularly painful.

I had been assigned to speak in sacrament meeting one Sunday afternoon in the spring of 1973. As I approached the Church building, I held on tightly to my handwritten notes as a soft ocean breeze tickled the pages. I straightened my red floral granny dress and tucked my long straight hair behind my ears. As I walked into the crowded sacrament meeting I was handed a copy of the program. It was still fragrant and damp from the old purple ditto machine in the Church library.

Without much thinking, I opened it up to see if they had spelled my name correctly. As I walked toward my seat on the stand, I was suddenly paralyzed.

Could there be some mistake? Oh, they had my name right. But how could it be that I was *one* of only *two* speakers? I was seventeen. A freshman in college. Living away from home for the first time. The only other talks I'd ever given in sacrament meeting were three minutes long.

Had I misunderstood when the invitation was offered? Or had no one mentioned the length? I expected to speak for about five minutes and had prepared accordingly. Another glance at the program revealed that the other speaker was another freshman—a shy 18-year-old young man, still months ahead of a mission call.

A sacred disaster was in the making.

The organist was playing prelude as I wobbled up to my seat and sorted through my notes. My heart was racing, my palms were sweating and my knees visibly shaking. Could a five-minute talk be stretched to last 30 minutes? Remember—this was back when sacrament meeting lasted an hour and a half. What choice did I have? I was willing to give it a whirl. I felt I simply had to *fill the time*.

I glanced over at my speaking companion and saw him nervously twisting a recent issue of the *New Era* into a tube. Before I had fully processed what was happening, the time came. I stood. I stammered. I stuffed. I stumbled. I stretched. And, eventually, I sat down. Oh, I filled the time; but I had not fulfilled my responsibility. I was devastated. I had failed myself. I had failed the ward. I had failed the Lord.

To the members of that sweet, forgiving ward in Orange, California, I must say: "I am truly sorry." Really. I still feel it more than 30 years later. It must have been the most excruciatingly painful sacrament meeting in history.

Each semester at Brigham Young University I teach dozens of students how to effectively organize and deliver their ideas to the public. I teach them how to do it all—business presentations, proposals, demonstrations, acceptance speeches, impromptu presentations, tributes and eulogies.

But I give special emphasis to speaking in sacrament meeting, mentioning it whenever I can. Of all their opportunities to speak, I tell them that sacrament meeting is one of the most sacred and should be cherished. Each sacrament meeting should be a spiritual experience.

Which brings me to the mission of this book—to help members develop, organize and deliver inspiring sermons in sacrament meeting.

Those who have never spoken in sacrament meeting will find help every step of the way—from defining the topic to final delivery. Those who have preached many times in sacrament meeting will discover hints to improve both their effectiveness and their confidence. If you happen to be facing the opportunity to speak in the immediate future, there are guidelines throughout the book that will assist in the process.

The gospel is exciting, wonderful and true! Moving that testimony from within your heart to the spoken word in sacrament meeting is a challenge. May the ideas contained in this book help you to share your love for the gospel—granting you greater impact on your listeners and increased peace in your heart. And may the Lord bless you abundantly in your efforts.

How to Use This Book

Amen is not a traditional text on public speaking. That simply wouldn't work when dealing with the sensitive and highly spiritual issue of speaking in sacrament meeting.

The principles of effective public speaking, many of them tested over thousands of years, are certainly valid in a discussion of speaking at Church; but there is another layer—a spiritual one—that must be applied before employing those principles. The spiritual truths that accompany the time-tested strategies in this book combine to give anyone who speaks in Church the foundation they need to accomplish their assignment with increased confidence, spirituality and success.

Amen is designed with a busy lifestyle in mind. Compact essays which address specific topics are grouped into larger thematic areas. Each one is grounded in scripture and focused on increasing your ability to help build the kingdom through the words you speak. As you read and act upon the suggestions, you'll find yourself implementing President Hinckley's counsel:

"There is room for improvement in every life. . . . We can improve ourselves and while so doing have an effect on the lives of those about us."[1]

Choose the method which seems best suited to your needs.

Read *Amen* straight through. One option is to read the book straight through, a few essays at a time. Soak up the essential information and put what sounds new and useful into immediate use.

Read *Amen* to treat specific symptoms. Decide where you think you need some strengthening or additional training. Titles of the essays give you a good idea of the content and focus. Look for specific solutions to specific trouble spots.

Read *Amen* to generate ideas. If while in the process of preparing a talk you find you're stuck, you may find that reading one of the essays is just what you need to help you work through a snag. Allow yourself a follow-up brainstorming session.

Read *Amen* as a devotional book. Use it as a daily or weekly devotional resource, knowing that in addition to reading a scripture passage, you will be introduced to principles that will contribute to your ability to speak more effectively in Church.

Read *Amen* as a reference book. Improving your speaking style is an incremental process. Keep the book on your shelf to refer to as needed. When a speaking opportunity is presented you can more easily polish up your skills.

Make *Amen* your personal speaking resource by jotting notations in the margins, underlining key passages and highlighting skills you want to work on. Additional resources can be found at www.perihelionpress.com.

Note

1. "Each a Better Person," *Ensign*, Nov. 2002, 99.

Realize
Your Role in God's Kingdom

Behold, the kingdom of God is within you.

Luke 17:21

A Resounding Amen

We believe all the words which thou hast spoken unto us . . . we have no more disposition to do evil, but to do good continually.

Mosiah 5:2

It takes place almost every Sunday. A fellow member of the Church stands and delivers a sermon. You're inspired and you're motivated. As a result, you're ready to face the world for another week.

As simple as that occurrence may be, when placed in the context of most of Christendom, it's amazing.

Speaking in Church—standing and bearing solitary witness before others without academic training, certificates and degrees in religion—is one of the most extraordinary aspects of the kingdom of God. Without a paid ministry, it falls upon the membership of the Church to share in the responsibility of giving words of inspiration and motivation each Sabbath. In taking your turn at the pulpit, you help build the kingdom by delivering gospel instruction and strengthening members spiritually

What's it like to give a sermon that changes people's lives forever? As recorded in the early chapters of Mosiah, King Benjamin gave one of the most powerful sermons of all time. The event itself was one of the most astounding peacetime gatherings ever described in ancient America—

remarkable in magnitude, purpose and impact. The massive tower, the ocean of tents, the surging crowds, the anticipation of change—it was an ancient general conference with a single powerful speaker. The transformation of individual souls was phenomenal as they simultaneously experienced a "mighty change" and pledged themselves to obedience and faithfulness.

But if you read the record carefully, you begin to realize that the process was not the work of King Benjamin's oratory skills alone—it was a joint effort between King Benjamin and the Lord. King Benjamin prepared a magnificent address and delivered it with power. But the Lord prepared King Benjamin.

Both the message and the messenger were inspired of God. Those with prepared hearts were transformed by the message because it was accompanied by a confirmation of the Holy Spirit. At the conclusion of his sermon one can only imagine the resounding "Amen" that echoed through the valley of Zarahemla.

Although he lived another three years, as far as we know, this was the final public address of King Benjamin. What made it possible for King Benjamin to create and deliver such a powerful sermon? This brief list of King Benjamin's attributes gives a glimpse into what made him a great person, great leader and great speaker. These are attributes you can develop that will help you improve your effectiveness as a speaker.

- He read the scriptures, both ancient records on the brass plates (MOSIAH 1:3–5) and modern records on the small plates of Nephi (MOSIAH 1:6)
- He prepared his message in advance, including a written copy (MOSIAH 1:10, 2:8, 9)
- He commended the obedience and faithfulness of others (MOSIAH 1:11)
- He showed gratitude to God for all his blessings (MOSIAH 2:4, 19–22)
- He was a man of Christlike love, referring to the Lamanites as his brethren (MOSIAH 2:5) and his own people as friends, brethren and kindred (MOSIAH 4:4)
- He was humble (MOSIAH 2:11, 12, 16–17)
- He served others as evidence of his love for the Lord (MOSIAH 2:17–18)
- He loved God (MOSIAH 2:28)

- ✦ He spoke in spite of physical limitations (MOSIAH 2:30)
- ✦ He preached the gospel (MOSIAH 2:31–41; 3:9–13, 25–27) and testified of the coming of Christ (MOSIAH 3:2–20)
- ✦ He knew what the Lord wanted him to say and he obeyed (MOSIAH 3:23)

The sermon of King Benjamin lived on long after he delivered it. Ammon taught the words of King Benjamin to the people of Limhi (MOSIAH 8:3). Almost 100 years later, inspired words from that sermon (MOSIAH 3:17) were quoted by Helaman in counsel to his sons Nephi and Lehi (HELAMAN 5:9). Over two thousand years later, we still quote him today.

What Makes a Good Sermon?

By this I know that thou art a man of God, and that the word of the Lord in thy mouth is truth.

1 Kings 17:24

The phone rang early one Sunday morning. It was my 18-year-old son who was working a summer job in California. He whispered in a low, almost hushed voice, that he needed to know something. "Mom, how do you make French toast?" I chuckled at the almost secretive manner in which this was being discussed. I guess he didn't want his roommates to know that he didn't know how to make French toast.

Once the recipe was revealed, I described how to determine when the French toast was fully cooked and ready to eat. Though you might come up with different adjectives, I would say that good French toast is crispy, cooked-through, warm, chewy, aromatic, tender, fluffy and buttery. Maybe the descriptors don't seem to make perfect sense—but when they all come together on the griddle it's a perfect breakfast. And that's exactly what my son was hoping for.

Describing a great talk in sacrament meeting is just as elusive, if not more so. You know when you hear one, but you may not be able to put it into words. Think of a sermon that left a lasting impression or made you feel you had feasted at a spiritual banquet. What made it memorable?

The following adjectives are an attempt at describing what kind of talk ward members are hungry for when they come to Church. Use them to motivate you to a higher standard when you are called to speak.

Inspiring. The carefully chosen scriptures and illustrations you use reach into the heart and touch your audience deeply.

Organized. Your introduction lays out where the sermon is going and then you proceed to that destination without delay. Your points flow in a sensible order that is easy to follow.

Refreshing. Your sermon contains new and delightful ideas, avoiding the predictable, overused or cliché.

Magnetic. You use stories, examples and ideas that draw the audience into your sermon and help them sense the importance and urgency of your message. The love you have for your listeners adds special appeal.

Focused. You have a clear mission, which is fulfilled by the thoughts you share. You make certain that your message brings your listeners to a deeper relationship with Christ.

Profound. The ideas you share get below skimming the surface of the gospel and hit at the most important truths of eternity.

Energetic. Your delivery shows you are alive and that you believe what you are saying. Your testimony is delivered with enthusiasm and rings with sincerity.

When you deliver your talk, ward members will feel they have been truly nourished. "Feast upon the words of Christ; for behold, the words of Christ will tell you all things what ye should do" (2 NEPHI 32:3).

Let Your Light Shine

For who will hearken unto you in this matter?

1 Samuel 30:24

Why does it seem that an invitation to speak often comes right after a splendid sacrament meeting? A meeting filled to the brim with motivating messages.

You may be inclined to compare yourself to the speakers you just heard and think, "What light could I shed on the subject I've been assigned? Do I really have anything to say?" Truthfully, you are of greater value than you realize.

On my first backpacking trip at age 13, the most memorable lesson I learned is just how dark night can be. As the sun disappeared behind the hills, darkness melted over the unfamiliar surroundings like hot fudge. Dead flashlight batteries only multiplied my awareness. With absolutely no source of light, the darkness was impenetrable. Every little crackling sound became a ferocious bear or ravenous mountain lion in my mind. Then, at about two AM, the moon rose: a glorious, reflective, light-giving orb. As she peaked over the mountain ridge, I drank in her amazing luminescence. As I glanced down, I was surprised to find I cast a shadow. The light gave me hope until morning. Did the moon know what a gift she was giving me?

When preparing to speak in sacrament meeting, you may be tempted to minimize the significance of your efforts or wonder if anyone will take you seriously. When you underestimate your potential influence, it makes the thought of speaking in sacrament meeting a little less uncomfortable because you've convinced yourself that it doesn't really matter that much. Nothing could be further from the truth.

What you do really matters. It matters to the ward. It matters to the Lord. And it matters to you. It matters because what you're doing is spreading holy light. In a world filled with darkness, your light matters immensely. Take counsel from the Savior: "Let your light so shine before men, that they may see your good works, and glorify your Father which is in heaven" (MATTHEW 5:16).

All you have to do is recall some of the talks, firesides and lessons that have helped shape your testimony to realize that essential truths, shared in simplicity, can illuminate the heart forever.

Respond with Gladness

He that receiveth my servants receiveth me.

Doctrine and Covenants 84:36

It seems harmless enough. A member of the bishopric stops you in the hall at Church and strikes up a casual conversation—kids, callings, schedules. Before long the topic migrates to family vacations and the fact that, yes, you will be in town next week. Speak in sacrament meeting? But . . .

At that exact moment what would you normally be feeling? A bit anxious? Join the throng. Tempted to offer a spontaneous excuse for your sudden unavailability? You're not alone. But what if you knew the invitation to speak in sacrament meeting were from the Savior? Ultimately, it is. "Whether by mine own voice or by the voice of my servants, it is the same" (D&C 1:38).

Once you can honestly accept the idea that the invitation to speak is from the Savior, your attitude toward the opportunity changes. The Savior knows both your strengths and your weaknesses and has invited you, in your imperfect and flawed condition, to address members of His flock. He has faith in you. And He expects you to have faith in Him.

Questioning one's ability and adequacy to speak is nothing new. The first record in the scriptures of someone with these same doubts is Enoch. "He bowed himself to the earth, before the Lord, and spake before the Lord, saying: Why is it that I have found favor in thy sight, and am but a lad, and all the people hate me; for I am slow of speech; wherefore am I thy servant?" The Lord responded with assurance, "Go forth and do as I have commanded thee. . . . Open thy mouth, and it shall be filled, and I will give thee utterance" (MOSES 6:31–32).

Another example of self-doubt is Moses. He explained to the Lord that the children of Israel wouldn't listen to him. "They will not believe me, nor hearken unto my voice. . . . Lord, I am not eloquent, neither heretofore, nor since thou hast spoken unto thy servant: but I am slow of speech, and of a slow tongue" (EXODUS 4:1, 10). The Lord rebuked Moses saying, "Who hath made man's mouth? Or who maketh the dumb, or the deaf, or the seeing, or the blind? Have not I the Lord? Now therefore go, and I will be with thy mouth, and teach thee what thou shalt say" (EXODUS 4:11).

In a Church staffed with a lay ministry, it's sometimes easy to forget that leaders serve with little formal training. Most of us inch along in our callings with on-the-job training, learning as much from our missteps and stumbles as from our giant strides forward. Asking someone to speak in sacrament meeting is no easy task. The risks are significant for the asker—rejection, miscommunication, offending or misunderstanding. Be sensitive to the difficulty of your priesthood leader's task also.

You may be asked in person or in writing or you may even get the invitation on your answering machine. Regardless of the method of conveyance, the invitation must still be seen as coming from the Lord. Once that hurdle is overcome, it's time, like Saul of Tarsus, who, when he finally recognized the voice of the Savior, said, "Lord, what wilt thou have me to do?" (ACTS 9:6)

Lifelong Preparation

Speak the thoughts that I shall put into your hearts . . .
For it shall be given unto you in the very hour,
yea, in the very moment what ye shall say.

Doctrine and Covenants 100:5

With a twist of his torso and a crack of the bat the baseball flew high into the grandstands. The crowd cheered as the runner jogged from base to base. It all looked so easy, almost choreographed. Yet, in a recent article describing the "10 Hardest Things to Do in Sports,"[1] hitting a baseball pitched at over 90 mph was listed as number one. How could something so difficult look so easy? For that baseball player it was more than just having a *gift*—it was the result of a lifetime of preparation.

In much the same way, some people can stand with almost no notes and deliver a powerful and inspiring sermon. Should that be your goal? To be honest, for most it is unrealistic. Not impossible, but unrealistic. Be careful of comparing yourself to seasoned speakers, but you should be willing to learn from them.

Two factors play into the equation that generates their greatness—persistent study and frequent speaking.

Persistent Study. To be able to produce results that way, you really have to be immersed in the scriptures every single day. That's why Church leaders and Church educators seem to be able to rattle off scriptures at the drop of a hat. Morning, noon and night they study the scriptures seeking ideas, insights and inspiration. Their callings require it and they are blessed because of it.

For the rest of us, though our study may be meaningful and devoted, passages are not always *at the ready,* to be called upon at a moment's notice. We are familiar with them, but cannot cite them spontaneously and accurately. You may find that you know where to look for a story or passage, but the details may have faded since your last study. You can reach a similar level of knowledge and fluency if you are willing to pay the price.

Frequent Speaking. Repeated trips to the pulpit place the speaker in the refiner's fire, mentally and spiritually. Those who are called upon to speak on a regular basis become more capable in the proficiencies that create a great speaker and a great sermon. They learn from the things that work—and also from those that don't. Then, piece by piece, a style of effective speaking and preparation develops. Their apparently spontaneous inspirational sermons are the result, in large part, of their service to the Lord which includes frequent opportunities to speak.

Most members of the Church speak in sacrament meeting rather infrequently. The solution is to benefit from the words, ideas and examples of those whose entire lives are devoted to the Lord and His gospel.

Note

1. *USA Today,* Feb. 18, 2003.

Finding the Answers

For thou wilt light my candle:
the Lord my God will enlighten my darkness.

Psalm 18:28

As you allow your topic to sink in, your mind will inevitably be flooded with questions. If it's a topic that is unfamiliar to you, your questions will be basic and lead you to an essential fundamental understanding. If it is a topic discussed frequently, your questions should lead you to a deeper knowledge with fresh insights valuable to you and listeners. In each case, the questions represent that which is unknown and deserving of further examination.

The Lord will lead you to the resources you need to answer your questions. Most of the revelations contained in the Doctrine and Covenants are a result of questions the Prophet Joseph presented to the Lord. His answers can be our answers also. It takes time, faith and an open heart to receive what it is the Lord has prepared for us. Write down your questions and begin your quest for answers.

Voices from the Past: Scripture

Moroni asserts that the scriptural record he was leaving behind would be "as one speaking from the dust" (MORONI 10:27). The pages of inspired accounts contained in the standard works reveal man's potential for both greatness and depravity, as well as the unchangeable love God has for all. But the pages become as useless as a "sealed book" unless they are opened and read. It's positively spine-tingling to discover a less-mentioned story in the scriptures that addresses the exact topic you want to discuss. It can only be found with diligent searching. Follow up cross-references which may take you to less frequently quoted passages.

Voices from on High: Still Small Voice

The key is to ask and then wait. Our minds and spirits are powerful receiving devices. But interference from competing voices may make it difficult to receive the intended message from the Lord. Turn off the TV, radio, CD player, computer and telephone. Give yourself some quiet time. Some alone time. Some uninterrupted time. Frame the question specifically and expect to be inspired. Write down impressions as they come—they need to be captured immediately or they could be lost. What you learn may not be something that demands mentioning in your talk, but it could be something designed just for you because you were willing to ask.

Voices from around Us: Connections

By discussing your topic openly with others, you may receive a new insight or a new way of dealing with the topic you've been studying. You may learn of others' struggles, temptations or victories. Other times the inspired people around you will merely present you with further questions. Those questions may redirect your thinking and allow you to catch a refreshing glimpse from a different direction. You will always strengthen your ideas when you listen to the ideas of others.

A Blessing in the Burden

Cast thy burden upon the Lord,
and he shall sustain thee.

Psalm 55:22

I remember the first time I carried a backpack. It was a wooden frame green canvas Army-style backpack, probably from World War II, though it was so battered it could have been from World War I. The narrow straps which dug into my shoulders were made of heavy cotton webbing which had no padding. My flannel and canvas sleeping bag must have weighed ten pounds. I remembered lugging canned foods and clanking canteens of water. I weighed less than a hundred pounds; my backpack over 25. To all this, add stiff Army surplus boots that were far larger than my feet and you had a blistered disaster waiting to happen.

But the thing that struck me as I trudged up the mountainside was that I was actually going somewhere important. I was headed to a place that was completely inaccessible to all but the truly committed—a place of incomparable beauty and serenity. When I arrived, I laid down my backpack and felt a supreme sense of accomplishment. No one else in the world had to know that I did it. I knew it. God knew it. And that was enough.

Whining about the pain would actually have diminished the victory, so I kept my bites, bruises and blisters to myself. I marveled at the beauty that only those who went into that wilderness would ever see.

For whatever reason, a tradition of grousing about speaking in sacrament meeting has arisen. It seems inconsistent that we would complain, even in jest, about one of the most remarkable opportunities that we as Saints are given. Eternal vistas are revealed to view when on the mountaintop of the Lord. A place you can only go with your heavy backpack and heavy responsibility. When you complete the assignment, you will have a supreme sense of accomplishment. You will know what it took—dragging a heavy weight up a mountain, to marvel at the beauty only those who go into wilderness will ever see.

Teach Truth

Speak ye every man the truth to his neighbour.

Zechariah 8:16

The combination lock is a fascinating device. In order to open the lock, the dial must be turned to a precise number. Finding the first one will take you to the next level, where equal precision must be employed. Eventually, if all numbers have been located exactly, you'll be able to open the lock. There is no room for fiddling with the order of the numbers or settling for being pretty close. Accuracy is the only path to success.

The gospel is true. Those called upon to proclaim the gospel from the pulpit have a profound responsibility to teach truth—pure, sound, true gospel doctrine. The gravity of the responsibility increases the amount of preparation that is required.

Ask yourself these questions as you prepare to carry out an assignment to speak in Church:

Do I know the truth? Study the word of God regularly—both the scriptures and the words of modern prophets. Find a study method that works for you. President Howard W. Hunter recommended that members set aside a certain amount of time for daily study rather than rushing through a specific number of pages. He observed that "sometimes the study of a single verse will occupy the entire time."[1] Methodical, serious study lays a powerful foundation for remaining faithful to the truth. Pay attention in Sunday school, Relief Society, priesthood, sacrament meeting and general conference. Schedule every possible opportunity to learn true principles.

Do I have a testimony of the truth? Be careful of relying on the testimonies of others. Having a solid testimony motivates you to stay true. Heber C. Kimball warned the Saints in 1856 that the time would come when "no man or woman would be able to endure on borrowed light."[2] Seek confirmation of principles that are new to you. Once you have a testimony in place, live what you know to be true.

Do I share the truth? Don't hide your light under a bushel; speak boldly of eternal principles. Speaking the truth influences others in unseen ways as the Holy Spirit confirms what you've said is true. The message is ultimately greater than the messenger.

Do I testify of the truth? Understand the essential parts of a testimony and bear solemn witness of the truths that have been revealed to you. Bearing testimony allows the Holy Ghost to further strengthen your conviction.

Scrutinize the words you plan to speak; make certain they are words of truth. Your responsibility to be a bearer of truth is a solemn one. President Gordon B. Hinckley stated: "I have spoken before about the importance of keeping the doctrine of the Church pure, and seeing that it is taught in all of our meetings. I worry about this. Small aberrations in doctrinal teaching can lead to large and evil falsehoods."[3] The Savior's expectation of those in the last dispensation is clear. "And I give unto you a commandment that you shall teach one another the doctrine of the kingdom" (D&C 88:77).

Notes

1. *The Teachings of Howard W. Hunter*, ed. Clyde J. Williams (1997), 53.
2. Orson F. Whitney, *Life of Heber C. Kimball* (1945), 450.
3. *Teachings of Gordon B. Hinckley* (1997), 620.

Build Testimonies

I commend you to God, and to the word of his grace, which is able to build you up.

Acts 20:32

I grew up around the construction industry; sawhorses, scaffolding and a cement mixer decorated our side yard year round. As a child, I understood that my dad played a part in making buildings; but I also knew he didn't do it all. He showed me the part that he did and explained how it added to the beauty, strength and longevity of the building. He also let me know that he always did his best. He wanted to be remembered as one who made any building he worked on stronger and better.

As you speak in Church, you will become a builder known for the quality of your work and the results you achieve.

Building the testimony of others. That's what you do from the pulpit—you contribute to the building of testimonies. You approach the task with the right words, the right ideas and the right attitude. You begin the task with a clear purpose in mind. When you bear solemn witness of an eternal principle, the Spirit confirms the truth of your words to those who are prepared to hear. That builds *their* testimonies.

Building the testimony in your heart. The added bonus comes when you actually speak the words you prepared. Because you approached the task with the right words, the right ideas and the right attitude, you will be inspired to communicate in a way that affects you as well as your listeners. The Spirit will confirm to you that what you have said is true. That builds *your* testimony.

The process of building yourself and those around you through inspired words is a valuable task. The evidence of your efforts, like those of a construction worker, will be all around you and will last for generations.

Build Relationships

I say unto you, be one;
and if ye are not one ye are not mine.

Doctrine and Covenants 38:27

At girls' camp one year we stood in a circle and talked about the importance of unity. Then a leader pulled out a ball of bright yellow yarn and tossed it to someone standing across the circle. She said something positive about the young woman and asked her to hold on to the yarn and toss the ball to someone else. The ball of yarn was slowly unwound as it bounced from girl to girl. Each contributed a kind word about the girl to whom the ball was being tossed. Soon there was a web of connection that was visible, tangible and understandable. I felt connected to each person in the circle. No one was an outsider.

The process of building unity within your ward is more than just words—it is a defining characteristic of followers of Christ. Ward members will feel more connected to you by your speaking, and you will feel more connected to them through your preparation to deliver something of value to them. The easiest way to build relationships as you speak is to connect using your eyes, words and heart.

Connect with your eyes. It is tempting to write out the *perfect* sacrament meeting talk and then just stand and read it. The dilemma is that ward members want to connect with you and feel that you are talking *with* them, not reading *to* them. The more they can see your eyes, the more connected they feel. You will also feel connected to them. As you look into their faces they will show their love and support, which will feed you and give you the strength to continue.

Connect with your words. Choose your words carefully. Words can be divisive or unifying. Using *we, our* and *us,* can be a positive way of connecting and saying to the members of the ward, "We're all in this together." Even when attempted in a humorous way, it can be hurtful to point out the faults and flaws of others. It's far better to find positive examples, especially within the ward. Find reasons to compliment ward members for their goodness, charity and sacrifice.

Connect with your heart. Before you speak, imagine the ward hearing your talk. Imagine the beneficial impact your message will have on them. Think about how much you love them. Prepare to deliver the talk in a way that conveys your tenderness toward them and shows your concern for their spiritual well-being.

When your eyes, words and heart simultaneously convey the message that you care about the members of your ward, both you and they will feel "Ye are no more strangers and foreigners, but fellow citizens with the saints, and of the household of God" (Ephesians 2:19).

Build the Kingdom

Go ye therefore, and teach all nations . . .
and, lo, I am with you always, even unto the end of the world.

Matthew 28:19–20

Across the street a new home is being built. Every day a variety of contractors and construction workers converge with their tools and equipment. However, the home is not being constructed from scratch—it is being built on an existing foundation. This new home will be bigger, better and stronger than the one that previously occupied that spot. But the new owner of the property is benefiting immensely from the solid foundation already in place.

In much the same way, we build the kingdom of God by building upon the solid foundation left behind by those who came before. We aren't building from scratch.

The apostle Paul saw the efforts of many contributing to the kingdom. "As a wise masterbuilder, I have laid the foundation, and another buildeth thereon. But let every man take heed how he buildeth thereupon. For other foundation can no man lay than that is laid, which is Jesus Christ" (1 Corinthians 3:10–11).

Building the kingdom of God in anticipation of the Second Coming of Christ is a responsibility that falls upon all members. When the opportunity to preach in sacrament meeting comes, if viewed within the light of the Savior's commission, the contribution is serious business requiring full attention to every detail.

The Lord declared, "Preach, exhort, declare the truth, even with a loud voice, with a sound of rejoicing" (D&C 19:37). Look closely at the words of the scripture—the call is to *preach, exhort* and *declare*—words of focused energy with a clear mission.

Since we're building through our words, we may need to reconsider how we think about and even talk about the experience of speaking in sacrament meeting. If we're going to build something of enduring value, we're going to have to abandon the notion that we are merely speaking or giving a talk.

President Gordon B. Hinckley observed, "Great buildings were never constructed on uncertain foundations. Great causes were never brought to success by vacillating leaders. The gospel was never expounded to the convincing of others without certainty. Without certitude on the part of believers, a religious cause becomes soft, without muscle, without the driving force that would broaden its influence and capture the hearts and affections of men and women."[1]

Note

1. *Stand a Little Taller* (2002), 98.

Prepare
Your Heart and Mind

Therefore, prepare thy heart to receive and obey the instructions which I am about to give unto you.

Doctrine and Covenants 132:3

Seek the Spirit

And when they had prayed . . .
they were all filled with the Holy Ghost,
and they spake the word of God with boldness.

Acts 4:31

Before you leave on vacation it's customary to fill the tank with gas. Clear up to the top. It feels good to start with a full tank. But after four or five hours behind the wheel, you notice the needle pointing toward "empty." You don't want to run out of gas, but you don't really want to lose time on the road just to fill up the tank. You want to get to your destination. The only problem is—if you run out of gas you'll never get there.

Much the same can be said about seeking the companionship of the Holy Ghost. It's easy to start out prayerful and contrite when the topic and content is uncertain and undeveloped. But as soon as the talk is written, you may not see focused prayer as such an essential part of the process. In reality, the Holy Ghost should be your partner each step of the way—from preparation, through delivery, through post-speaking wrap-up.

To ensure that your sermon has the desired effect on ward members, the Holy Ghost must be present when you speak. The preparation for having the Holy Ghost accompany your message starts long before you stand in sacrament meeting. It starts from the moment you accept the assignment.

Pray as you prepare. Seek the guidance of the Spirit as you accept your assignment. You may be startled at the unexpected directions the Lord can lead you. Be prepared to be submissive.

Pray over the topic. Discover what topic the Lord wants you to address. The process of prayerfully selecting and narrowing the topic is essential. If you take a wrong turn at this point in the preparation, it is harder to get back to where you need to be. Get on the right track and the Holy Ghost will confirm it in your heart.

Pray about the mission statement. As your topic is narrowed and the direction made clear, you then prayerfully draft a mission statement. Once you draft it, edit it, modify it and prune it—then use it. Everything you choose to include will be measured against that standard. The Holy Ghost will help you uncover what the ward needs to hear from you.

Pray as you research. Don't assume that the first scripture story or general conference address dealing with your topic is the one you should select. Be open to guidance from the Spirit. Follow a chain of scriptures as you check out the footnotes at the bottom of the page. Sometimes a lesser-known story can actually be more effective in making a specific point. Look for ideas which are spiritually refreshing.

Pray over your sermon writing. This is deliberate writing, not stream-of-consciousness. Once you have your mission firmly planted in your heart, you begin the delightful process of research and sifting. You read a general conference talk. You check in your journal. You follow a scripture chain. You read the newspaper. You look in the LDS Bible Dictionary. The process is exquisitely inspired and inspiring. You find things you didn't know existed. You find new meanings in passages you have loved for years—all because you asked the Lord to help you in the writing process. The Holy Ghost will lead you to resources and help you select the best. Don't discount any direction your writing takes you. Include the Lord in your final editing—what you choose to take out is as important to the final product as what you leave in.

Pray over your delivery. Before you walk up to the pulpit, your heart should be drawn out to the Lord. This is not *your* sermon, it belongs to Him. Pray that you will deliver it in such a way as ward members will receive the message that you have prepared. Your efforts to respond to the promptings of the Holy Spirit will be rewarded with a distinct and indescribable feeling of doing something significant with the help of the Lord. Expect peace. It will come. The Holy Ghost will grant you the strength to complete the task you have been assigned.

Pray as you reflect. When it's all over, you may want to breathe a sigh of relief and put it behind you. However, this can actually be one of the sweetest moments as you reflect on how the Lord guided you in each step of preparation and delivery. If you feel you grew from the experience, a prayer of gratitude would be an appropriate conclusion to the experience.

Each word of prayer will draw you closer to the Holy Spirit and make it possible for you to follow the pattern established by the Apostle Paul: "We speak, not in the words which man's wisdom teacheth, but which the Holy Ghost teacheth" (1 CORINTHIANS 2:13).

Four Lessons from the Savior

In the morning, rising up a great while before day, [Jesus] went out, and departed into a solitary place and there prayed . . . And he said unto them let us go to the next towns, that I may preach there also: for therefore came I forth.

Mark 1:35,38

Many assume that Jesus, being the Son of God, stood and delivered eloquent and quotable sermons spontaneously. This belief deserves thoughtful examination. If the Savior learned "line upon line, here a little, there a little," then it would be reasonable that, like us, He would need to carefully organize His thoughts before speaking. And that always takes time. In the midst of His many good works, the Savior found time to collect His thoughts before speaking to the multitude.

There are four lessons that can be learned from this brief mention of the Savior's preparation before speaking.

Morning hours are valuable. All hours are not created equal. Anyone who has ever heard birdsong at dawn knows that nature recognizes the difference between sunrise and sunset. Morning is often equated with the Resurrection, with the rising of the sun recalling the rising of the Son. The world is reborn every morning with the return of daylight. Find some early morning hours for contemplation and reflection.

Solitude is essential. The Savior was surrounded by throngs every day. Many loved him. Some hated him. All were curious about this great man who was able to feed thousands, heal the sick and calm the sea. To prepare to share a message of purity and power, He needed to be refreshed—He needed to be alone. Find time to be alone.

Quiet is important. The clanging, clattering and chattering that surrounded the Savior all day—even when they were voices of adoration—made inner peace less accessible. For us, it can shut out the whisperings of the still small voice. Find a quiet place where interruption is impossible, and you'll find a place where revelation is possible.

Prayer is the foundation. The Savior knew His role in the kingdom of God, and yet He needed to communicate with the Father to receive the direction He needed before speaking to His growing number of followers. How much greater is our need for guidance from on high. Find time for focused prayer.

Seven Questions

What shall we do,
that we might work the works of God?

John 6:28

Often it comes out of the blue. "Will you speak in sacrament meeting next week?" It's such a simple question. But it has a ten-ton brick attached to it.

When you're invited to speak in sacrament meeting, you may be a little startled by the invitation. Feeling both flustered and flattered, you probably agree to speak. But do you have all the information you need? Don't overlook gathering crucial information in your enthusiasm to serve.

The following seven questions can smooth out the process. Some of the information will be given to you when the call is issued. If so, write it down. You'll probably find it useful to collect the information sought by these questions—either at the time of the invitation or in a follow-up call.

It is the responsibility of priesthood leaders to select topics for sacrament meeting talks and to select and orient participants. The priesthood leader who invites you to speak will be grateful you are trying to learn as much as you can regarding his expectations. If you are invited in writing, follow up with the priesthood leader who is named as your contact. Having this information will help you to manage your time, set your course and serve more effectively.

1. On what date will I be speaking? Make sure you heard the date accurately, then check your calendar carefully. You may want to look at the days leading up to your assignment. Determine what flexibility you have in your schedule in order to open up sufficient time for preparation.

2. How long should I speak? Get a specific time limit or range, if possible. Commit to using the amount of time given for your sermon—no less, no more. You can expect to need one hour of preparation for each one minute of speaking. To help you plan your remarks more efficiently, know that most speak at a pace averaging about 120–150 words per minute.

3. Is there an assigned topic for me? If you are given a broad topic, ask for guidance on how to narrow it further. Determine if there is a desired outcome. If there is no assigned topic, you may want to ask for a suggestion as a starting point.

4. Is there a theme? Knowing what general subject will connect the various talks will allow you to blend with the overall theme of the meeting, allowing the messages to seem more naturally linked. It will also build your confidence as you feel part of a greater whole.

5. What other topics are being addressed? Knowing the other assigned topics will help you avoid stepping on others' topics. It will also help clarify how to more effectively address yours. You will be able to narrow your topic with greater assurance that your message will fit in. Be sure to discover if all speakers have been given the same topic.

6. Who else is speaking? It can help to know if you are speaking with five other ward members, a returning missionary or a member of the high council. If you are familiar with their styles, this can help. You can also contact them prior to speaking to identify their approach to the topic or theme. You can then more easily connect without fear that you'll overlap or duplicate.

7. Where do I come in the program? Determine whether you are the first speaker, the concluding speaker, speaking right in the middle or after a musical number. By chatting with the speaker or musician who precedes you, connections can be made that will give your message greater impact. Also, being the final speaker requires the most flexibility, as you may need to shrink or stretch your sermon should previous speakers go short or long.

Asking these questions, and using the answers, will help you create an inspiring sermon that will make a difference and fit in smoothly with the overall message of the meeting.

Seven More Questions

Thou hast not asked riches, wealth, or honour . . .
but hast asked wisdom and knowledge.

2 Chronicles 1:11

The right questions stimulate your thinking processes, pushing you into issues which might be overlooked otherwise. These questions are designed to help you prepare a message specifically created for the ward members you will speak to. Use the questions for a spiritual brainstorming session.

1. What is my topic? To get started with the process, list every possible topic, subtopic and or related subject. Select the topic that will work best. Narrow your topic to a manageable size.

2. What is my mission? Identify what you want to accomplish as you speak to this specific audience. Write down what you want them to know, do, feel or believe when you are finished speaking.

3. What is my message? Determine what you want to say about your topic. Develop a clear angle or position. You can't say everything, so choose to say something memorable and valuable. Your goal is to package one clear concept for listeners to remember and take home.

4. **Who is my audience?** Consider age, background, ethnicity, education, length of time in the Church, family, employment, local situations and anything else that might affect the way you develop your sermon content. Write your talk with your specific audience in mind. Consider how your topic has been previously discussed by ward members—in classes, over the pulpit and in private conversations. Remember, you are addressing your brothers and sisters.

5. **What is my experience with this topic?** On a piece of paper, list significant experiences you've had with your gospel topic: talks you've heard, books you've read, promptings you've received, situations you've seen, lessons you've taught and scriptures that stand out. Meaningful ideas can bubble to the surface as you think about your life experiences. Don't stop writing until you feel you covered everything.

6. **Where can I look for additional insights?** Start with the scriptures and recent general conference addresses, then branch out to find ideas, quotes, hymns, poems, essays and insights which expand, strengthen, clarify or assist with the application of sacred principles.

7. **What does the Lord want me to say?** Most importantly, prayerfully discover what the Lord needs you to say. Be open to taking an unexpected path as the Holy Spirit guides you.

These seven questions are an effective starting point toward the creation of an inspired message. "When a man speaketh by the power of the Holy Ghost the power of the Holy Ghost carrieth it unto the hearts of the children of men" (2 NEPHI 33:1).

Make Haste

I made haste, and delayed not to keep thy commandments.

Psalm 119:60

Unlike the digital, hyper-speed, instant-response electronic world most of us live in, there is an element of patience and preparation that comes with the workings of the Spirit. The unhurried pace of the Holy Ghost may seem somewhat contradictory to the urging to *make haste*. Actually, the reason you need to make haste is because of the patience required. From the moment you receive the assignment, you begin the process of prayerful preparation.

The shepherds visited by angels on the night of the Savior's birth understood the importance of acting immediately. There were probably steps they needed to take to secure their flocks before they could leave. But they made the necessary arrangements and were witnesses to one of the most celestial scenes on earth. Had they delayed, they might have missed it. "The shepherds said one to another, Let us now go even unto Bethlehem, and see this thing which is come to pass, which the Lord hath made known unto us. And they came with haste, and found Mary, and Joseph, and the babe lying in a manger" (Luke 2:15–16).

Make haste to receive heavenly guidance. By immediately setting to the task and allowing the Lord to work with you, you will see positive results.

More focused topic. You will discover the best way to narrow your topic because you'll consider so many more options rather than grabbing the first that occurs to you.

Clearer mission. You will have a solid sense of what it is you're trying to accomplish and will find the best materials to that end.

Greater sensitivity to ward members. You will envision members of your ward and their relationship to this topic, finding ways to specifically bless them with your message.

Increased confidence. You will avoid the anxiety that accompanies last-minute preparation. You will arrive at sacrament meeting confident that the message you have prepared will bless ward members.

Better delivery. Your voice will be stronger as you deliver a text with which you are comfortable. You will have time to smooth out troublesome sentences and become accustomed to your notes.

Starting earlier doesn't mean that you'll finish any sooner. It does mean that you'll be in better position to receive the light the Lord has prepared for you.

Cleanse Our Hearts

The Holy Spirit of God did come down from heaven, and did enter into their hearts, . . . and they could speak forth marvelous words.

Helaman 5:45

No matter how long you leave it in the oven—if you've added toxic ingredients you will never get an edible cake. How much arsenic are you willing to accept in your next slice of carrot cake?

As plain as that is to understand, there is cultural resistance to applying that concept to the ingredients deposited daily in our brains by those with dark and self-serving intentions, especially as it concerns music. God created our brains to be the most amazing information storage and retrieval systems ever. Scientists still marvel at what the human brain is capable of storing and processing. Yet with all its remarkable capacity, we allow dreadful stuff to enter.

In *For the Strength of Youth,* young people in the Church are counseled: "Unworthy music may seem harmless, but it can have evil effects on your mind and spirit."[1] The effects of inappropriate music can be just as harmful to adult members of the Church.

Consider how many hours a day you spend being pumped full of words and ideas that oppose principles of the gospel or deny the power of God.

Music has become as enveloping as the air we breathe, and in many cases more polluted. Sometimes the immersion is by choice and sometimes it's just the way things are, but awareness is the first step to making a conscious change.

As you glance at this list, notice how saturated with pop music your life and environment may have become. You may want to take deliberate steps to reduce your exposure and schedule some quiet. Do you:

Wake up to a music alarm?
Play music in the shower?
Dress to CD in bedroom?
Listen to music while making breakfast?
Get in the car and flip on the radio?
Check computer for latest movie trailers with soundtrack?
Go for a walk with MP3 player?
Have music playing at the workplace?
Work out at gym with exercise music?
Eat lunch at restaurant with background music?
Drive home with music in the car?
Shop at the mall with music in every store?
Watch a movie with a dozen pop songs in background?
Drift off to sleep with favorite CDs or radio playing?

Perhaps you only checked off half the items on this list. If you are feeling satisfied, you may want to ask yourself how many hours per day that represents. The number can still be alarming. There are two important reasons to reduce your exposure.

Lyrics are powerful. Not all lyrics are harmful, but how degrading does a message have to be to affect the listener in a negative way? Often the lyrics that are knit to pulse-pounding rhythms are designed to drive just a small wedge between you and the Spirit. Are you really willing to accept that?

Consider what's playing on the radio today. The language of modern music is often crude, profane, debased, and defiles the names of deity. The images created in the lyrics can be ugly and soul-tarnishing. The words often portray violence, vandalism, physical abuse, crime, deviant behavior, drug usage, alcohol abuse or pre-marital sex as acceptable steps into adulthood rather than the sins they are. Perhaps this is what Isaiah saw when he warned, "Woe unto them that call evil good, and good evil; that put darkness for light, and light for darkness; that put bitter for sweet, and sweet for bitter!" (ISAIAH 5:20)

Unconsciously allowing these lyrics to be drummed into your brain hour after hour, day after day, is sure to have an effect. When it's time to pull up ideas for a talk in sacrament meeting, if all that is stored in your brain are quotes from current movies and cuts from current songs, then your personal reservoir may be dangerously shallow.

Quiet is powerful. Create extended interludes of sublime silence. You will discover an atmosphere free of interference. Admittedly, complete quiet is rather difficult to secure in most environments; even in funeral homes there is background music. Life seems incomplete without an accompanying soundtrack. Without deliberately modifying your situation, it may be challenging for the "still small voice" to nudge you in new directions or give you specific guidance.

The absence of uninterrupted solitude could be spiritually endangering, as it is unfair to expect the Holy Spirit to compete with the cacophony of modern culture. Consider trying three days of a music-free and media-free existence. It could open up a whole new world of experiences and growth as well as reveal musical habits you need to amend. Some people feel uncomfortable with quiet, when compared to the pre-packaged life-soundtrack that has become the model. Try breaking free, so the Holy Spirit can more easily influence your life.

Note

1. *For the Strength of Youth* (2001), 20.

Christ-Centered Sermons

She saith unto him,
Yea, Lord: I believe that thou art the Christ, the Son of God,
which should come into the world.

John 11:27

In high school, I was no athlete. But in the 10th grade I discovered a sport I really enjoyed. I was never excellent, but at least I understood what the instructor wanted me to do. It was archery. The bull's-eye, right in the center of the target, was in plain sight. I knew if I am aimed for it I had a good chance of hitting it. If I didn't aim, I had no chance at all.

Christ is the central message of the gospel. All gospel messages ultimately lead us to the Savior and the Atonement. When asked about the foundational beliefs of the Church, Joseph Smith replied, "The fundamental principles of our religion are the testimony of the Apostles and Prophets, concerning Jesus Christ, that He died, was buried, and rose again the third day, and ascended into heaven; and all other things which pertain to our religion are only appendages to it."[1] This message has been echoed by every prophet since then.

One of the safest ways to proceed with any topic is to ask yourself Christ-centered questions. No matter what you are speaking about, you will always find Christ at the center of the topic. These three questions can help you collect ideas and insights.

What has the Savior said about this principle? Explore the words of the Savior carefully. Study those which are attributed directly to Him in the New Testament, Book of Mormon and Doctrine and Covenants as well as those He has inspired to be written by prophets and Apostles. Make certain that you understand what the Savior has said, so that when you repackage the idea within the context of today's environment the message remains consistent.

How did the Savior exemplify this principle? Reread stories of the Savior's life and find moments where He showed His feeling about the principle or how He lived it Himself. There were also situations where He skillfully helped someone come to an understanding of the principle through His questions. You can also look at how He tutored the Prophets.

How does living this principle draw me closer to the Savior? Every gospel principle transforms us, piece by piece, from the "natural man" to a "man of God." What will people know, do, feel or believe differently after experimenting with this principle?

Talks given in sacrament meeting are designed to draw listeners to a deeper relationship with the Savior. Whether you inspire, motivate or explain, make the Savior the source and the focus of your message.

Note

1. *Teachings of the Prophet Joseph Smith*, sel. Joseph Fielding Smith (1938), 121.

Fulfill Your Purpose

For verily this is a day appointed unto you to rest from your labors, and to pay thy devotions unto the Most High.

Doctrine and Covenants 59:10

As a child I was mesmerized by my mother's cabinet of rocks. She was known as a "rock hound" and had spent years collecting the vast array of specimens stored behind glistening glass doors. Although there were tags indicating the rare nature of some of the minerals, the one that captivated me was the golf-ball-sized hunk of gold. Pure gold. I was sure of it. My mother would remind me that it was actually iron pyrite, or fool's gold, but I was sure that we were wealthy beyond belief. It was golden and sparkly, so what else could it be?

The difference between gold, which has immense value, and pyrite, which is virtually worthless, is in the intrinsic qualities of the metals. Even though it has a golden hue to it, pyrite's structure causes it to be hard, brittle and dull by comparison. During the gold rush in California, many unsuspecting forty-niners found themselves with pouches full of fool's gold. Pyrite does not have the distinctive tarnish-free luster, brilliance, weight and malleability of pure gold.

The density and glimmer of gold makes it a pleasure to hold as coinage or wear as jewelry. Its unique qualities give it universal appeal. Gold, a stubborn element when it comes to reacting to or combining with other elements, is found primarily in slender almost-pure veins at various locations throughout the world. It is virtually indestructible, with almost all gold ever mined still in existence. Once you have felt the heavy, suppleness of gold and seen its incomparable gleam, you will never be fooled by the cheap imposter.

Sermons given in sacrament meeting need to be pure gold. The gold standard for sermons is to lead listeners to God. Regardless of your topic, all messages should lead to God. When planning to speak in sacrament meeting, it's helpful to remember the purpose of sacrament meeting. President James E. Faust counseled, "Our sacrament meetings should be worshipful and healing, restoring those who attend to spiritual soundness."[1] Although not all would recognize a sermon made of lesser content, your integrity demands a higher standard.

As hearts are turned to the Lord during the sacrament, your words should build on that same purpose. With that in mind, all topics—no matter how specific and narrow—should fall easily into one of the following broader themes that have a focus on our relationship with God.

- Love of God
- Commandments of God
- Church of God
- History of God's kingdom on earth
- Attributes of God
- Blessings of God
- Expectations of God
- Condescension of God
- Priesthood of God
- Godliness
- Power of God
- Communicating with God

- ✦ Godhead
- ✦ Creations of God
- ✦ Life with God
- ✦ God's plan of salvation

What you speak about should draw hearts to a more reverent feeling toward God the Father, Jesus Christ and the Holy Ghost. Examine the content of your talk against this gold standard. Then prune, chop and edit; rethink, refresh and rewrite. The result will be a talk that turns hearts, yours and ward members, to the Savior.

Note

1. "He Healeth the Broken Heart," *Ensign*, July 2005, 5.

A Strong Foundation

Built upon the foundation of the apostles and prophets, Jesus Christ himself being the chief corner stone.

Ephesians 2:20

The task, to design and construct a bell tower to adorn the cathedral of Pisa, Italy, was a worthy challenge for an artist such as Bonnano Pisano. In 1173, construction began on this architectural icon. He did not intend for the tower to lean. But after building just three stories, and at a height of 35 feet, it was noticed that the tower was beginning to sink unevenly into the water table just six feet below ground level. With five years invested in the project, the architect scrambled to devise a strategy to correct the obvious tilt of the tower. By raising the galleries on the side that leaned he fooled some. But the correction was little more than an optical illusion. Over the centuries that followed, the tower tilted further and further. The problem was the faulty foundation, not the elegant tower. The work of countless artisans was upstaged by the poor planning, leaving a tower that will be forever remembered for its angle rather than its artistry. Lacking a firm foundation, the Leaning Tower of Pisa has continued to shift to a point that in September 1995, it nearly toppled.

Sacrament meeting talks can suffer the same fate if not established on a strong and stable foundation. In order to build a solid base, your message must be anchored in the revealed word of God. The Savior established the pattern of relying on sacred words as He quoted from the prophets throughout his ministry, chastising those who did not know the scriptures. "Jesus answered and said unto them, Ye do err, not knowing the scriptures" (MATTHEW 22:29).

Before going out on a limb with your own opinions, make sure that you are not on shaky ground. We should not speak on subjects that are speculative, controversial or out of harmony with Church doctrine. Do your gospel homework.

Begin by asking yourself these three questions:

1. Where is this principle found in ancient scriptures?
2. Where is this principle found in modern revelation?
3. What have current prophets had to say about this principle?

Go to the fountain of truth and drink deeply of that pure and refreshing water. Establish your message in the word of God. Build a sure foundation.

The Three Components of a Sermon

And the great city was divided into three parts.

Revelation 16:19

Thumpah-thumpah-thumpah-thumpah. After a long hard run it's great to know your heart is still on-duty. Working hard. Doing its job. It feels great to take your pulse and realize how faithful your circulatory system is; oxygen is being transported to every cell in your body. When all the parts of the system are in working order, life is good.

The proper functioning of your circulatory system relies on specific structure, content and delivery to maintain life. The *structure* of the circulatory system is the heart and blood vessels. It is well organized and efficient, getting the blood from head to toe all day long. The *content* of the system is the blood—life-giving fluid that surges around bringing oxygen-rich cells to replace those which are oxygen-depleted. The *delivery* is the pumping action of the heart which assures that all dependent systems are benefited.

Structure, content and delivery in the circulation system keeps you alive. If any portion of the system breaks down, you're more than inconvenienced, you're dead.

In a sermon the life-giving components are also found in the structure, content and delivery. The success of the communication system is dependent on understanding each part and keeping all elements in balance.

Structure is the organization and flow of the message. Listeners appreciate having a sense of order, so they can tell where they are and where they are headed.

Content is the subject matter, focus and research which make up the ideas you will communicate. It needs to be meaningful to both you and your audience.

Delivery is the way the message gets from your heart to theirs. Your voice, word choices, gestures, facial expressions and pauses contribute to the meaning received by the audience.

If any component is missing or weak, the life-changing impact of the message may be impaired or diminished. Examine your speaking pattern and determine where you may need to be strengthened. Your message is more important than the oxygen delivered by blood—that only gives life. You bring the message of *eternal life*.

Be kind to yourself as you work on improving your skills in writing and delivering sermons. When the message is true and is anchored in holy writ, the Spirit intercedes to fill in many gaps that might exist in the mechanics of structure, content and delivery.

Listeners expect a sacrament meeting sermon to illuminate a gospel principle and to bless them with applicable knowledge. Considering the three components of structure, content and delivery will help you accomplish that goal.

LISTEN TO GREAT TALKS

Learn of me, and listen to my words;
walk in the meekness of my Spirit,
and you shall have peace in me.

DOCTRINE AND COVENANTS 19:23

LISTENING AND RE-LISTENING TO GENERAL CONFERENCE may be one of the most efficient and enjoyable methods to improve your abilities to write and speak. You've probably noticed that certain speakers generate within you a desire to do good, try harder and be more faithful. Other speakers bear a testimony that seems to speak directly to your soul. Still others have a power to lift you up and make you feel hopeful and optimistic. Certain speakers have such clarity of thought and command of language that you are immediately brought to a new and deeper understanding of a gospel principle. Of course, these are gifts. But they are gifts that are honed and magnified from repeated experiences at the pulpit.

Thanks to technology, there are many options for listening to general conference addresses—options that seem to be expanding daily. You can hear conference addresses on live television, satellite, radio or Internet broadcast, television replay, video on-demand from some cable suppliers, archives at www.lds.org, CDs, audio tapes, as well as MP3 downloads.

You may wonder why listening is important when the *Ensign* publishes a printed version soon after general conference concludes. It's because listening is a different process than reading. Unlike reading, which requires specific decoding skills and high attentiveness, listening allows for spirit-to-spirit communication and a more casual big-picture approach. While listening you can catch repeated phrases, nuances of interpretation or vocal emphasis that might not come through on the printed page. As the content and meaning of a general conference address becomes more discernible, your ability to see the style that made it so increases.

Consider a few questions to help you scratch beneath the surface:

1. How was the message organized?
2. How was the topic revealed?
3. How was the audience drawn into the subject matter?
4. Was there a story? If so, was it personal, historical or from the scriptures?
5. Did you feel inspired or motivated?
6. How was the message delivered?
7. How did the speaker keep your interest?
8. Were there new insights, ideas or information that left an impression?
9. How did the speaker conclude?
10. What made the message memorable?

It may seem odd to be analyzing general conference addresses. But studying great speakers who are also inspired is a remarkably powerful and valuable exercise. Twice a year we are granted the privilege of hearing from some of the most valiant and righteous on earth. These leaders have refined their communication skills in the fires of consecrated service. Who better to learn from!

THE SAVIOR'S FLOCK

I will feed my flock . . . saith the Lord God.

EZEKIEL 34:15

Spiritual Nourishment

It shall even be as when an hungry man dreameth, and, behold he eateth; but he awaketh, and his soul is empty.

Isaiah 29:8

Ward members come to Church hungry for the word of God. There is no time of the week when Saints are more fully prepared to receive counsel from the Lord than immediately following the partaking of the sacrament. The Lord's Supper reminds us of who we are and why we are here. President Spencer W. Kimball counseled priesthood leaders, "Every congregation is people hungering and thirsting for righteousness and our help and inspiration."[1]

A great opportunity is missed if a roomful of penitent and humble Saints are gathered and they do not receive inspired counsel. They are ready to receive nourishment from the full banquet of the gospel—not some empty-calorie, puffed-up, sugar-coated, breakfast cereal version. Feasting on the word of Christ is the most delicious and satisfying activity on any Sabbath. Yet with the feast so readily available, there can be surprisingly meager offerings some weeks.

The Savior warned of focusing on gospel minutiae and losing the chance to discuss "the weightier matters of the law" (MATTHEW 23:23). Sacrament meeting provides a rare opportunity each week for us to feed each other messages that will bless and nourish eternally. The followers of Alma were blessed by consecrated leaders and teachers who "did nourish them with things pertaining to righteousness" (MOSIAH 23:18).

Jacob, Nephi's younger brother, understood how delicious and satisfying the gospel can be when he said, "Come, my brethren, every one that thirsteth, come ye to the waters; and he that hath no money, come buy and eat; yea, come buy wine and milk without money and without price. . . . Feast upon that which perisheth not, neither can be corrupted, and let your soul delight in fatness" (2 NEPHI 9:50–51). When it comes to the word of God, there is no dieting. As a speaker, your commitment should be to provide the bread of life in generous portions to all who come ready and willing to partake.

Christ has warned, "I will send a famine in the land, not a famine of bread, nor a thirst for water, but of hearing the words of the Lord" (AMOS 8:11). A quick glance at what's available in the media today and you can see that prophesied famine spreading throughout the nation and the world. People are spiritually starving, religiously malnourished and morally famished. Elder Jeffrey R. Holland observed, "The gospel of Jesus Christ is the only way to satisfy ultimate spiritual hunger."[2]

Notes

1. *The Teachings of Spencer W. Kimball*, ed. Edward L. Kimball, (1982), 522.
2. "He Hath Filled the Hungry with Good Things." *Ensign*, Nov. 1997, 64.

Difficult Topics

We speak; not as pleasing men, but God.

1 Thessalonians 2:4

No one wants to be the person who delivers bad news. But pleasing God will always be your first duty.

There are times when difficult topics must be sensitively addressed in sacrament meeting. An additional layer of difficulty and discomfort comes with the territory when assigned a tough topic. Do not shrink from the responsibility, however prickly the problem. If the Lord has selected you as the messenger for such a message, spend even more time in the preparatory steps. Prayerful study will expand your understanding of complex issues and emotionally charged subjects.

As you come to appreciate the Lord's position on the topic, you will set words to paper that will be a blessing to the ward and fortify your own conviction. The awkwardness you may feel in discussing the issue will subside as you develop compassionate content and rehearse the toughest passages.

Development of your sermon may require consulting with your bishop if you have concerns on how to approach the topic appropriately. Both he and the Lord are expressing faith in your ability to convey the message with clarity by suggesting you take on the task. The message may be uncomfortable, but your bishop has determined that it's necessary.

Your assignment is not unlike that which faced the Book of Mormon prophet Jacob. He was grieved at the boldness he had to use in the presence of those "whose feelings are exceedingly tender, and chaste, and delicate before God." He would much rather have preached "the pleasing word of God . . . which healeth the wounded soul." Instead, Jacob wisely chose to follow the "strict commands of God" and tell the people "the truth according to the plainness of the word of God" (JACOB 2:7, 8, 11).

Standing at the pulpit, you may have a moment when pleasing God first means rubbing some Saints the wrong way. Be gentle but firm, using the example of the Apostles and prophets in the most recent session of general conference. Read their words and see how they deftly discourse on unpopular topics.

Pleasing God is a lofty but soul-satisfying goal. The dilemma of discussing difficult subject matter was mentioned by Elder Dallin H. Oaks following the April 2005 general conference.

> Last week I was talking with a member of the Quorum of the Twelve about comments we had received on our April conference talks. My friend said someone told him, "I surely enjoyed your talk." We agreed that this is not the kind of comment we like to receive. As my friend said, "I didn't give that talk to be *enjoyed*. What does he think I am, some kind of entertainer?"
>
> Another member of our quorum joined the conversation by saying, "That reminds me of the story of a good minister. When a parishioner said, 'I surely enjoyed your sermon today,' the minister replied, 'In that case, you didn't understand it.'"
>
> You may remember that this April conference I spoke on pornography. No one told me they "enjoyed" that talk—not one! In fact, there was nothing enjoyable in it even for me.[1]

The Apostle Paul was willing to speak boldly without concern for his popularity. Yet, in order for his message to have impact, listeners had to be drawn into the message and feel the love of God. Paul proclaimed the power of Christ's role in their lives before he offered counsel or instruction. His allegiance was to God first, but he loved those who wanted to follow God. He challenged the early Saints to serve God not "as menpleasers; but as the servants of Christ, doing the will of God from the heart" (EPHESIANS 6:6).

As you prayerfully work on your talk, you will be inspired as to what to say and when. Just remember that your obligation is to God first. The Savior has declared that "This is my work and my glory—to bring to pass the immortality and eternal life of man" (MOSES 1:39), so He will surely urge you to say those things that will draw people toward greater faithfulness in Him and His gospel.

Note

1. "The Dedication of a Lifetime," *CES Fireside for Young Adults,* May 1, 2005.

Love Your Listeners

Though I speak
with the tongues of men and of angels, and have not charity,
I am become as sounding brass, or a tinkling cymbal.

1 Corinthians 13:1

"My beloved brothers and sisters . . ." The love that President Gordon B. Hinckley has for members of the Church is felt whenever he speaks, echoing through every syllable. There are few things as comforting as being spoken to lovingly by someone who cares about you. You feel the warmth and connection. You know they are words that come from the heart.

As you seek for and are blessed with the pure love of Christ, you will naturally include information in your remarks that you believe will bless the members of the ward. When that is your motivation, your audience will feel it and respond positively. Tap into that power and see how it enhances how your message is received.

Be concerned for their happiness. Every audience member is concerned about being happy and finding the path that leads to happiness. Show that you are truly happy and want to share your experiences in the gospel that have brought you the most happiness. Let them know when you are teaching a principle that has happiness attached to it.

Be concerned for their well-being. Physical health, mental health and spiritual health are often intermingled in the scriptures and are bound by eternal laws. Show that you care that the audience feels well by sharing your insights on maintaining your well-being through obedience to the revealed word of God.

Be concerned for their relationship with God. While in mortal probation most do not see God, but all have access to God. Show that you want to help strengthen their relationship through teaching about prayer and the ordinances of the gospel.

Be concerned for their eternal joy. In the midst of the trials of mortality, it is not always easy to see the path that leads to eternal life. In Lehi's vision of the tree of life, there were many who lost their way in the mists of darkness, drifted away and were lost. Show that you care about their eternal salvation and want them to be blessed forever through the gospel of Jesus Christ.

There is no component of your speaking that is more important than having the pure love of Christ. It will touch every person who listens to you. "Wherefore, my beloved brethren, pray unto the Father with all the energy of heart, that ye may be filled with this love" (MORONI 7:48). It is a gift of the Spirit that must be sought, and when received will bless you and those to whom you speak. Your concern for others will be natural, warm and sincere.

A Sermon's Power

And after I, Enos, had heard these words, my faith began to be unshaken in the Lord.

Enos 1:11

Never underestimate the power of an inspired and well-delivered sermon. Whether delivered by an angel or by an angelic member of the ward, a heaven-sent message can motivate the prepared heart to make a lifesaving course correction. There are unknown difficulties facing members of the ward family that your inspired message may help resolve. There are broken hearts, rebellious spirits and troubled souls. There are also those who just need a word of encouragement.

In my ward there is a wonderful young man in a family of high-achievers. Everything David does—academically, athletically, spiritually—has always been of the highest caliber. He has been in the ward since the age of 14 and seemed to be headed straight for his Eagle rank in Boy Scouting. But somehow he got sidetracked and started losing enthusiasm, even when he was very close to finishing.

A man in the ward gave a brief but powerful talk on the meaning of commitment, mentioning that the Lord expects us to follow through on our promises. This man had been David's Scoutmaster during his early days of

Scouting. Suddenly, the right words, at the right time, in the right way, lit a fire under this young man. Within a matter of days he had a project started, final merit badges wrapped up, paperwork completed and his Eagle rank achieved.

It is impossible to measure the value of a timely idea delivered with energy and conviction. In most cases, we never see the outcome. It could be months or even years after the fact. We serve with faith that our effort will make a difference.

Communicate with Love

By this shall all men know that ye are my disciples,
if ye have love one to another.

John 13:35

Ebenezer Scrooge, the curmudgeonly character we all love to hate, wins us over in the end as we see his phenomenal transformation from selfish hermit to ebullient benefactor. Just thinking about the conclusion of the story makes you want to smile. We love him because we can see love finally emerging from his closed-off heart. We love being loved. We yearn to be loved. And we listen most closely to those who speak with love.

Smile. The easiest way to communicate love is through a simple but sincere smile. Since speaking in sacrament meeting is an infrequent opportunity for most, nervousness can snatch the smile that would normally spread across your face. This may seem odd, but it can be quite helpful to practice smiling. Even if the only time you can muster a smile is before you start speaking, look up at the ward members and smile broadly before you glance down at your notes.

Eye contact. We expect that people who love us will look into our faces. Prepare sufficiently so you can look into the eyes of the ward members awaiting your message. They want to feel connected to you and to your message.

Word choice. The words you choose really can make a difference. The warmth of a well-turned phrase, the depth of a well-crafted idea and the insight of a fully developed sermon shows love and concern that is always appreciated.

Show your love through your preparation. Be prepared with a smile, a friendly look and well-prepared message. Your love will come shining through.

The Golden Rule

Whatsoever ye would that men should do to you, do ye even so to them.

Matthew 7:12

As you glance over the printed program on Sunday and notice who is speaking, you probably wish them well. You can easily imagine them giving an outstanding sermon—one with well-prepared content, inspiring ideas, fresh insights and passionate delivery.

When the tables are turned and you're the one speaking in sacrament meeting, it's easy to lose sight of what the ward members may be expecting. Stop and imagine what it would be like to hear your own talk. As a way of showing your love for your ward members, hold yourself to a high standard.

Remember—it's not about you, it's about them. You already know the information that you intend to share. Your job now is to prepare and deliver it such a way that their lives are blessed. That is the same purpose you hope they undertake when they speak to you.

Well-prepared content. Take the time to develop content that shows you studied the topic carefully and extensively. It's easy to jot down the first things that come to mind as your main points, but this may keep you from digging more deeply into the issue. Remain open to both new insights and new information as you prayerfully explore.

Inspiring ideas. Over the years, everyone has a mental list of favorite general conference talks—ones that really moved us to make giant strides spiritually. These can be a great resource for inspiring concepts that can frame a sacrament meeting talk. Mark up your conference issues of the *Ensign,* so you can easily find those great messages again.

Fresh insights. When considering your topic be sure to ponder how it has played out in your own life. It's possible that how you've applied a gospel principle and the outcome you experienced would be especially helpful to someone else. Although great care has to be taken in what is revealed from the pulpit, positive outcomes are almost always inspirational. Should you have any concerns, be sure to discuss it with your priesthood leader.

Passionate delivery. Whatever you create on paper, remains meaningless and flat until you bring it to life at the pulpit. Once you have a spiritual conviction that what you have to say is important, then you need to communicate with passion. Those who speak with passion have the power to send their message directly from heart to heart.

If you can keep the Golden Rule in mind as you create your message, the audience will feel that the focus is on them and their needs.

What If I'm Boring?

*And there sat in a window a certain young man named Eutychus,
being fallen into a deep sleep:
and as Paul was long preaching,
he sunk down with sleep, and fell down from the third loft,
and was taken up dead.*

Acts 20:9

The thought of being boring is terrifying. You know what a terrible thing that is to inflict upon ward members. Your speaking, regardless of any supposed inadequacies, is unlikely to produce the near-fatal results it had with Eutychus (Paul miraculously brought him back to life). Still, no one wants to look out from the pulpit to a sea of slumbering Saints.

How do you avoid this? Find your passion, or deepest feeling, within the topic you're developing.

Focus your sermon with passion. Discover and then write down, the single most important message you want ward members to have as a result of your talk. You may want to post it in large letters near where you will be practicing so you don't lose your focus. Remind yourself daily, even when you're not actively working on your sermon. Your passion will grow.

Write your sermon with passion. Seek out from the best sources for the support you need for this message. Find a variety of sources so you have plenty to choose from. As you begin to define your main points, the best possible examples, stories, scriptures and hymns will naturally emerge.

Deliver your sermon with passion. Break out of your comfort zone and *declare your message,* rather than simply read your talk. Make it come alive with the passion you feel. Proper preparation—prayer and practice—will allow you to deliver the most powerful message.

Each person communicates their passion in a different way—so just because you are not a pulpit-pounder doesn't mean members of the ward will drift off to sleep. Conveying the deep feeling you have through your voice, your words, your facial expression and your testimony will awaken within them sympathetic feelings toward your message. They will be spiritually enlivened as a result of listening to you.

Praise Ward Members

Let another man praise thee,
and not thine own mouth.

Proverbs 27:2

As you develop the content of your sermon, you may find you have certain predictable patterns of research that you implement. And there's certainly nothing wrong with continuing to use an efficient model. However, there is something fresh and energizing about trying something new.

One of the first places we look for examples is our own lives. Good plan. But it can get tiresome if you're always the hero in every inspirational story. Is there someone else who could be blessed by walking in the limelight for just a moment? Have you heard an inspiring story within the neighborhood? Within your extended family? Within your ward? There is goodness all around us, acts of bravery, charity, sacrifice and service that exemplify the best within us all. And behind every act of goodness, there is a story.

Collect the details. The more details you have, the more believable the story is. Don't go overboard, but give enough details that listeners can imagine being there.

Describe the motivation. Uncover the motivation this person had to accomplish this virtuous act. Sometimes people don't know why they did something and that is a story also. Try to learn about their lifestyle, personality and spiritual gifts.

Outline the obstacles. No good deed proceeds without significant stumbling blocks. The adversary of all righteousness never sleeps. Learn what was overcome to make the remarkable result possible. In your storytelling, this is the ideal place to create emotional tension as it seems the barriers are insurmountable. Give sufficient detail that a pleasant resolution is in doubt.

Reveal the outcome. In good storytelling, you try to maintain the tension of an unresolved conflict as long as possible. Maintain uncertainty that can only be managed with ultimate faith. The conclusion will be splendid and memorable as the hand of the Lord is seen through the Christlike acts of others.

All right, it does take a little more effort to uncover the inspirational story in someone else's life than it does to dig one up out of your own. But it's worth it. Consider the impact of telling about the goodness of people around you. It can only generate more goodness. And that's a pretty good reason to start speaking in the first place.

We Are All Temporary

Neither were there Lamanites, nor any manner of -ites;
but they were in one, the children of Christ.

4 Nephi 1:17

Divisions among the family of Christ, even minor ones, almost always create unnecessary problems and hurt feelings. One avoidable dilemma that poses a problem in many wards is the temporary member—one who is here today and gone tomorrow. Guess what? That's all of us. Each funeral reminds us of that.

Education, medical needs, military service, specialized job training, internships, sales positions, seasonal work and temporary employment can cause anyone to go through a season of impermanence. A ward family can create a sense of belonging and a feeling of stability in an increasingly instable world.

As you speak in sacrament meeting, treat yourself and others as solid, permanent members of your ward. The boundaries of Church units are not eternal in nature, but membership in God's kingdom is. Perhaps it would be easier to think of transient members as long-lost relatives that are only seen at family reunions. Rejoice every time they worship with you.

It doesn't matter if a ward member is a graduate student, temporary worker, summer vacationer, foreign visitor or member of the armed forces. There is room for everyone. The dynamic nature of a ward family involves making adjustments and including each person. We adjust for missionaries . . . let's adjust for everyone else. Almost all relationships in a ward are somewhat temporary in nature, but they require us to think long term.

When speaking, tune into the eternal and universal yearnings of the soul. The Savior was the supreme example in modeling this. If you think about His three-year ministry, you realize that Jesus traveled from town to town, never staying long enough to set down roots. Yet, everyone who met Him felt an immediate kinship. It's not difficult to imagine being a member of the family of Christ; He is our Elder Brother.

Now, expand this in your speaking. We are all members of the family of Christ. Some of us are on vacation, some of us are just passing through, and some of us are more established. But we all need each other—every brother and sister.

Think of the faithful ones who received Christ at the temple at Bountiful—they became one as they grew in the pure of love of Christ. "And how blessed were they!" (4 Nephi 1:18)

Time Is a Gift

And the Lord appointed a set time, saying,
To morrow the Lord shall do this thing in the land.

Exodus 9:5

If you knew this would be your final week on earth, you would expect people to be respectful of honoring the limited time you had remaining in mortality. What if you knew you had only 35 years left? Would your time be any less valuable?

With good cause you expect others to respect your time. You show the audience respect by how you use their time.

What do you owe your audience when speaking in Church?

Truth. A sermon that shows respect teaches true principles. Like an orchestra that is perfectly in tune on the sounding of the first chord—a true message will resonate in every heart.

Diligence. A sermon that shows respect is hard work. There's no repackaging that verity. But your hard work will result in well-researched and well-developed ideas that you will enjoy delivering. Be sure to give the ideas of others proper attribution.

Preparation. A sermon that shows respect takes serious preparation. Rehearsal makes things go more smoothly for the speaker, but it also benefits the audience. They receive a better presentation, with more expression, that is less likely to have accidental mistakes or misquotes.

Honor. A sermon that shows respect demands that you honor the time you're given. No stretching allowed. No wincing when the clock runs out. Prepare to honor that sacred trust.

The Sacred Trust of the Pulpit

When you stand to speak you have been entrusted with something valuable and completely irretrievable—the time of the members of your ward. It is of great value, perhaps more than you suppose. Let's take a standard 12-minute sermon. The time spent speaking represents a simple 12 minutes out of your life (although it may feel like much more). However, when that same 12 minutes is multiplied by the total number in attendance, a more accurate picture is revealed. If there are 200 members attending sacrament meeting, your responsibility would more accurately be calculated as follows:

12 minutes x 200 people = 2400 minutes ÷ 60 = 40 hours

or the equivalent of 5 full work days
devoted to hearing your message

From the very outset, commit to work within the allotted time. Whether you are working from a manuscript or an outline, you can easily predict how long a talk will take. If you're speaking from a manuscript where every word is written out, plan on 120–150 words per minute. Using the word-count feature on your word processor or by hand-counting you can find your total. Either way, if you've been given 12 minutes, there is no way that you can deliver more than about 1,500 words. If you're working from an outline, it will take you several practices to determine if you can work within the time you've been given.

Once you understand the principle behind the Sacred Trust of the Pulpit, the time you're given increases in significance. Going overtime, even just a few minutes, suddenly takes on much larger proportions. Further, your doing so deprives other speakers of sharing what they have prepared and the audience of hearing their full message.

Those few minutes behind the pulpit are a sacred trust; use them well.

Carve Out Time

Do not procrastinate the day of your repentance until the end.

Alma 34:33

I WANTED FRESHLY BAKED BREAD to go with the soup I had made. I knew that I'd have to plan ahead in order to give the bread time to rise. Setting the cookbook out on the counter, I dreamed of the luscious aroma that was going to fill my kitchen. While I grabbed the mixing bowl from the cupboard, the phone rang and I was momentarily distracted. The phone call reminded me of another commitment and I dashed out the door. On the way home, I stopped to return an item I had borrowed and got into an animated discussion with a neighbor. When I returned home, I saw the pieces on the counter but there was no time left to do anything but serve saltines.

Familiar scenario? Sure our lives are already full with wonderful things. *Finding time* is an impossibility. *Making time* would be miraculous. *Carving out time* is about all we can hope to do. Make sure you carve out enough from your full week.

Since you probably do not speak in sacrament meeting that often, you probably have not developed a routine for writing, researching, pondering and rehearsing. The big surprise is that it takes more time than you think.

Plan about one hour of preparation time per minute of speaking. Maybe that seems extreme to you now, but when you actually begin the task it may start to seem insufficient.

As you accept a speaking assignment, make sure you allow enough time to prepare. A 20-minute sacrament meeting sermon, from scratch, may take 20 hours to prepare, including prayer, scripture study, research, organization, multiple drafts and rehearsal. Determine if you have sufficient time to research, draft and practice your sermon. "For which of you, intending to build a tower, sitteth not down first and counteth the cost, whether he have sufficient to finish it?" (LUKE 14:28)

Fear of Hypocrisy

Every one is an hypocrite. . . .
For all this his anger is not turned away,
but his hand is stretched out still.

Isaiah 9:17

It's nice to know the Lord can love a hypocrite. Ultimately, absent of perfection, we each struggle with a degree of hypocrisy. We preach principles we are not yet fully living. That is the nature of mortality. Fortunately, that doesn't change the value of the principle. We teach the principles we know are true and are striving to live. The key is to do so in humility.

What is a hypocrite anyway? As used most frequently in the New Testament, a hypocrite is one who puts on the appearance of being more virtuous or religious than they really are. It comes from the Greek word *hypokrites* for actor or pretender. The Savior condemned hypocrisy repeatedly.

With any degree of introspection you may be thinking that you are not living a particular gospel principle well enough to preach about it—that to do so would land you squarely in the camp of the hypocrites. Well, if that were the case, the only one who could ever address us would be the Savior. Knowing your weaknesses and flaws, He still calls you to testify of Him and His gospel.

Preaching is a powerful way to expand and deepen commitment to a commandment. With the companionship of the Holy Ghost testifying of its eternal truth, casual observance can be replaced by renewed devotion and dedication. As we strive to avoid unrighteous judgment of others, we should also be compassionate with ourselves.

The journey is long and the obstacles many—but heaven is still the destination of all who enter the strait and narrow path and endeavor to live faithfully.

Search

for Sacred Ideas

Search the prophets,
for many there be that testify of these things.

3 Nephi 23:5

SOURCES OF TRUTH

Jesus answering said unto them,
Do ye not therefore err,
because ye know not the scriptures?

MARK 12:24

WE COME TO SACRAMENT MEETING to be taught eternal truths. Truth should be found in abundance in every talk given. As you search for truth you will discover that some sources will always be a better than others. We should always begin with the best.

Elder Neal A. Maxwell observed, "There is an aristocracy among truths; some truths are simply and everlastingly more significant than others! In this hierarchy of truths are some which illuminate both history and the future and which give men a realistic view of themselves—a view that makes all the difference in the world."[1]

Unless exquisitely worded, most of your research will end up as paraphrased ideas or snippets of information. Give attribution when appropriate as it will increase credibility. Keep in mind that available resources are immense, so limit your search to the few that will best serve your purpose. Your research should enhance your knowledge, fortify your faithfulness and deepen your testimony.

This hierarchy of support is created with the counsel of the Brethren in mind. Choose the best resources possible. It can be deceptively easy to construct a sermon based on hearsay, flimsy evidence and poor research. But the impact of a well-developed sermon can be everlasting, if the heart of a listener is stirred to a remembrance of the Savior and the principles of the restored gospel.

First Tier

You should always cite at least one of these sources in your sacrament meeting sermon. This is where you begin your search for ideas and inspiration. Of course, just because you start here doesn't mean you end here.

- ✦ Holy Bible (including the Joseph Smith Translation), Book of Mormon, Doctrine and Covenants, Pearl of Great Price (actual passages as well as paraphrased stories)
- ✦ Recent general conference addresses of current prophets and Apostles (available in May and November issues of *Ensign* and online at www.lds.org)

Second Tier

As you continue your search, you can feel generally safe using ideas from these sources. Most have been through priesthood correlation and are cited regularly by the general authorities. It can be helpful to find different discussions of the same issue to secure your understanding.

- ✦ Personal experiences (from memory or from your journal; be selective and sensitive to what is appropriate)
- ✦ *Gospel Essentials*
- ✦ *For the Strength of Youth*
- ✦ *True to the Faith*
- ✦ *Hymns of the Church of Jesus Christ of Latter-day Saints* (1985)
- ✦ *Children's Songbook* (1989)

- LDS Bible Dictionary (from the 1981 LDS Version of the King James Bible)
- *Ensign* articles (Note: General conference issues are in the first tier)
- *New Era* articles
- *LDS Church News*
- Current Church manuals and handbooks (in use)
- Scriptural footnotes, cross-references, chapter headings
- Conference addresses of past prophets and Apostles
- Church history and Church historical documents
- Text from speeches, devotionals, firesides given by general authorities
- Personal observation (observing others)
- Parable/metaphor/analogy/simile/allegory (as used in the scriptures or your own creation)
- Personal research or interviews tied directly to the gospel topic
- Counsel from local Church leaders

Third Tier

As you deepen and expand your research, be judicious in using ideas from these sources. The risk of error or conjecture slipping into your sermon increases and the sources have less connection with revealed truth. There are still valuable ideas that can be collected and effectively used from these resources.

- LDS research and archaeology
- Non-LDS Bible dictionaries, encyclopedias, concordances or lexicons
- Other translations of the Bible
- Non-fiction books by Latter-day Saint authors
- *Deseret News Church Almanac*
- Firsthand stories from others' lives
- Your personal notations in scriptures

- ✦ News reports (verifiable, not rumors)
- ✦ Journal articles, scientific studies, research
- ✦ Non-sacred quotes from quote books or on-line sources
- ✦ History and biography
- ✦ Poetry
- ✦ Hymns from non-LDS hymnals
- ✦ Great literature which exemplifies a gospel principle
- ✦ Encyclopedias, dictionaries

Note

1. *The Smallest Part* (1973), 4.

The Dictionary Is Our Friend

A word fitly spoken is like apples of gold.

Proverbs 25:11

Sacrament meeting is not the place for a stodgy vocabulary lesson. There is really no reason to ever begin a talk with "Webster defines *consecration* as . . . " First of all, Webster doesn't own the definition to any word. That collectively belongs to all of us. So if you want to tell the meaning of a word, just go ahead and blurt it out. "Consecration is . . . " Quoting the dictionary is completely unnecessary. And for most spiritual topics, the standard dictionary is incomplete, shallow and sometimes misleading.

However, the dictionary can be our friend, adding depth of understanding and increasing your confidence. Always have one at the ready when you start drafting your sacrament meeting talk. Learning from the dictionary is far more valuable than quoting from it.

Pronunciation. The dictionary can give you the preferred pronunciation of any unfamiliar word. This one step can keep you from erasing previously established credibility. If you have any doubt about the pronunciation of a word, look it up. English is too unpredictable to assume anything about pronunciation.

Meaning. Understanding the most widely held meanings of a particular word can be helpful, especially if the word is used slightly differently in a spiritual context.

Connotations. Discovering the more complete array of meanings a word might have will keep you from using *mongrel* when you meant to use *purebred.*

Word history (etymology). Sometimes the most significant information about a word is its history. Discovering what language the word migrated from and what the meaning was anciently can shed new light and can add depth to your discussion.

Synonyms. Overusing one single word in a talk can become tedious. Find any existing synonyms that can be exchanged from time to time. It adds both clarity and interest.

A standard collegiate dictionary is a good place to start. You can find more information on-line as well as in subject area dictionaries available at the public library. And don't forget the fabulous additional resources in the LDS Bible Dictionary.

USE WELL-KNOWN LITERATURE

Become acquainted with all good books, and with languages, tongues, and people.

DOCTRINE AND COVENANTS 90:15

WHEN PAUL STOOD AMONG THE GREEKS in the midst of Mars' hill, he said, "Ye men of Athens, I perceive that in all things ye are too superstitious. For as I passed by, and beheld your devotions, I found an altar with this inscription, TO THE UNKNOWN GOD. Whom therefore ye ignorantly worship, him declare I unto you" (ACTS 17:22–23).

Paul knew the stories and legends and myths that were widely known among the people of Athens. By using the reference "To the unknown god," he was able to create a common ground from which to build his sermon. The same strategy can be undertaken to teach concepts and principles today.

There is a wide assortment of universally known characters and narratives from which brief examples can be drawn. Although culturally unnerving to contemplate, there are probably more people in America who are familiar with the characters of *The Simpsons* than are familiar with the characters of Shakespeare. But for sacrament meeting, the ideal is to identify a story, character or situation that is widely known and from which a credible point or instructive example can be made.

Consider ways in which great authors' works have been used at general conference to illuminate gospel principles:

William Shakespeare. The universality of Shakespeare's themes and the timelessness of his language still enthrall listeners today. President Thomas S. Monson frequently and masterfully includes the words of Shakespeare's plays and sonnets in many of his addresses. Speaking on the power of example and quoting from *Two Gentlemen of Verona,* he said "How do you honor your parents? I like the words of William Shakespeare: 'They do not love that do not show their love.'"[1]

C. S. Lewis. Known for his beloved children's books, Lewis was also a magnificent Christian theologian. *The Screwtape Letters* is Lewis' telling of a senior demon, Screwtape, who sends instructions to his apprentice, Wormwood, on how to best tempt mortals. It provides readers with delightful insights on the workings of Satan. Elder Neal A. Maxwell cited Screwtape in describing the folly of "those who go dashing back and forth with fire extinguishers in times of flood."[2]

Charles Dickens. President Hinckley enjoys the vivid characters and language of Dickens. In describing the evil and persecutions which accompanied the Restoration of the gospel, he recalled the opening line from *Tale of Two Cities*: "It was the best of times, it was the worst of times . . . it was the season of Light, it was the season of Darkness, it was the spring of hope, it was the winter of despair."[3]

For stories which are not widely known, it can be helpful to clarify that they are fictional before starting. As you use material from great literature, fables, mythology, current fiction or even fairy tales, make sure listeners understand the point you are trying to make. It is essential to maintain the dignity of sacrament meeting, so if you are the least bit doubtful about a choice from fiction, look elsewhere.

Notes

1. "Be Thou an Example." *Ensign,* May 2005, 112.
2. "Remember How Merciful the Lord Hath Been," *Ensign,* May 2004, 44.
3. "The Dawning of a Brighter Day," *Ensign,* May 2004, 81.

The Savior Used Scriptures

Jesus saith unto them,
Did ye never read in the scriptures,
The stone which the builders rejected,
the same is become the head of the corner?

Matthew 21:42

The Savior used the scriptures of the Old Testament abundantly in His sermons. The stories, ideas, concepts and phrases were oft-repeated cultural focal points that could easily be referred to. The more familiar the story, the more He could use the equivalent of scriptural shorthand to speak to a gathering.

A good example of this is found in the early days of the Savior's ministry, when He healed many as a manifestation of His role as the long-awaited Messiah. "That it might be fulfilled which was spoken by Esaias the prophet, saying, Himself took our infirmities, and bare our sicknesses" (Matthew 8:17). His comment refers to the well-known messianic prophecy in Isaiah 53.

Scriptural shorthand doesn't always work. The secular environment of 21st century western culture makes it more difficult to call upon lesser-known passages and expect universal understanding. However, that doesn't mean that they can't be effectively used. It's a matter of giving listeners enough information to appreciate the interactions of the characters, their particular adversities, and the spiritual lesson that can be learned.

Set the stage. Describe the details that are known, both those recorded in the scriptures and those that are known from concurrent historical texts. Information about the location can be instructive also.

Identify the characters. Focus on those who play a role in the story or situation you're describing. Draw a defining line between good and evil, faithful and faithless.

Illustrate the conflict, problem or issue. Help listeners sort out what is happening that needs to be discussed by defining and describing the situation clearly.

Make your point. Even scripture stories need someone to point out the significance and application of the story. Some narratives have multiple meanings and interpretations—choose and underscore the one that works for you.

The more often that scriptures passages are fully and deeply discussed in sacrament meeting, the more often these sacred stories will be ingrained into our collective memory.

Avoid Rumors

Satan did stir them up to do iniquity continually; yea, he did go about spreading rumors.

HELAMAN 16:22

"HEY, DID YOU EVER HEAR THE ONE ABOUT . . ." Although very few sacrament meeting talks begin the way you might start a joke, it's surprising how often a talk may find a "tall tale" woven in. It seems harmless enough. After all, it has a "ring" of truth. But sacrament meeting is not the place for passing along half-truths or hoaxes.

The gospel is already so miraculous and astounding that it doesn't require embellishment with stories of questionable origin.

President Harold B. Lee spoke sternly of rumor "which, when once started, gains momentum as each telling becomes more fanciful, until unwittingly those who wish to dwell on the sensational repeat them in firesides, in classes, in Relief Society gatherings and priesthood quorum classes without first verifying the source . . . causing speculation and discussions that steal time away from the things that would be profitable and beneficial and enlightening to their souls."[1]

President Lee went on to refute a rumor about a patriarchal blessing he was alleged to have received with details about the second coming of the

Savior. What he found most shocking was that those who heard the rumors were disappointed to find they were not true. He said "they seemed to have enjoyed believing a rumor without substance of fact."[2]

President Lee concluded: "It never ceases to amaze me how gullible some of our Church members are in broadcasting these sensational stories, or dreams, or visions, some alleged to have been given to Church leaders, past or present, supposedly from some person's private diary, without first verifying the report with proper Church authorities."[3]

It is tempting to retell a story that seems inspirational, but is of unknown or spurious origin. Stories of this nature abound on the Internet. If you don't have personal knowledge of the reality of the story, and therefore cannot with any degree of certainty substantiate it, your credibility slips, and the righteous desire of your heart to influence others to do good, may be misdirected.

Notes

1. "Admonitions for the Priesthood of God," *Ensign*, Jan. 1973, 104.
2. Ibid.
3. Ibid.

Who Said It?

He said unto them,
But whom say ye that I am?

Luke 9:20

"Oh, yeah—says who?" In spite of the deplorable grammar, no child has escaped hearing this at least once. This common playground taunt underscores how important it is to establish from whom a statement comes. We never really outgrow this model, although we tend to be more subtle and discreet in our response.

Whenever you quote someone—a current Church leader, someone from the scriptures, a leader in the early days of the Church, a great thinker—the audience needs to know why they should take that person seriously. Silently running through the minds of those listening to you may be any of the following:

- Can I trust this person?
- What was their relationship to God?
- Do they have insights that would be valuable to me?
- How were their experiences similar to mine?

- ✦ Do they have authority over me?
- ✦ Do they have my best interests at heart?

Giving relevant insight into the person, even just briefly, elevates the likelihood of their counsel or insight being received positively.

In the New Testament, the words of Paul are quite different from the words of Peter. How did their personal experiences cause their insights to be different? Where can you look to find information about them? Sometimes it is just as valuable to make someone seem particularly human as it is to make them seem especially good.

Get to know the author of any quote you share. Then make sure your audience is introduced to that person also. You don't have to tell them everything you know, but don't assume they will accept counsel from a stranger. What follows are some brief biographical notations that reveal a few of the unique characteristics and experiences of Peter and Paul, especially those which could have influenced why they said or wrote certain things.

Peter: One of the first followers of Christ with his brother Andrew, his name means "Rock," fisherman, Galilean, present at the Transfiguration of Christ, married, hard-worker, impetuous, walked with the Savior, denied Jesus three times prior to the crucifixion, presided over the early Christian Church, held the keys of the kingdom, opened the gospel to the gentiles, most likely source for the Gospel of Mark, probably martyred in Rome, conferred the Melchizedek priesthood upon Joseph Smith and Oliver Cowdery.

Paul: Formerly known as Saul of Tarsus, trained as a Pharisee by Gamaliel, tentmaker, Roman citizen, persecuted and executed Christians, on the road to Damascus struck blind and heard the voice of the Savior, sight was restored, converted to Christianity and baptized by Ananias, survived a shipwreck, stoned, had a vision of Christ, performed miracles, wrote 14 epistles, devoted follower of Christ whom he never met, almost converted King Agrippa, was most likely martyred by being beheaded.

Mark the Scriptures

For who hath stood in the counsel of the Lord,
and hath perceived and heard his word?
who hath marked his word, and heard it?

Jeremiah 23:18

Have you noticed that when you glance down at a page of unmarked scriptures, all the verses look alike? Add the stress of standing at the pulpit and it becomes increasingly unlikely that you'll be able to find the pre-selected scripture passage you wanted to share. Consider some of these ideas in marking your scriptures to assist you in your personal study as well as speaking.

Use more than one color to mark your scriptures. You probably notice many passages that are meaningful and deserve to be marked. But an ocean of red is generally no better than an unmarked page. Multiple colors allow you to easily see the beginning and ending of the thought you were trying to capture.

Mark only part of a verse. Don't feel compelled to mark every word or color in the whole boxed scripture. Sometimes it can be helpful to underline certain words or phrases. Other times, it may just be the quotation contained within the verse. Maybe it is the question that is asked that is most important. Often, you can find the real "meat" of the scripture by skipping over "And it came to pass . . . " and similar phrases. Sometimes there are two distinct and valuable thoughts in a single verse and you may need to use two different colors to identify those. After a verse is colored in and you want to add extra emphasis, you can use a pen to underline specific words.

Vary the marking technique. No need to color in solid every single time. You can box in a scripture, leaving the center white. You can run a line down the side of a story that takes up numerous verses. You can use diagonal hash-marks. You can use large bracketing to capture a story or event. Write a notation at the top of the page indicating what the main focus of the large passage is.

Create personal footnotes and cross-references. Use a fine point pen to jot down ideas that deserve to be recorded in the scriptures. This can be a personal revelation or insight. It can be a translation note. Historical information can be helpful. Referencing other resources may assist you in research for a talk. Cross references that are not listed at the bottom of the page that you have found insightful should definitely be included.

Identify seminary scripture mastery and missionary verses. It can be informative to know which scriptures have been selected by Church leaders to be taught in seminary and at the Missionary Training Centers. The universality of the message and the familiarity of the texts can be important.

Mark, note and date. When you have a particularly poignant experience with a scripture passage, mark it, make a notation and date it. It will make returning to that spot all the more meaningful. This will make your scriptures a record of your personal experience with the word of God.

Well-marked scriptures are helpful at the pulpit as the precious passages are so much easier to find and quote accurately.

Great Thoughts

He pronounced all these words unto me with his mouth, and I wrote them with ink in the book.

Jeremiah 36:18

In 1989, a young Hindu scholar from India stayed in our home for a week. We invited Dinesh to attend Church with us and be introduced to our beliefs and form of worship. He was gracious in accepting our invitation and prepared himself for the experience. During sacrament meeting, a 12-year-old Beehive was the youth speaker. About 30 seconds into her talk, our guest pulled out a small journal from his pocket and jotted something on the pages. I later asked him what he had written down. It was a gospel principle that I had long taken for granted, but was fresh for my friend. Dinesh said, "Whenever I hear something profound, I write it down so I can make the lesson a part of my life."

The question that arose in my mind was why I wasn't doing the same thing? Dinesh had come expecting to receive something worthwhile and was prepared to retain it.

Sitting in sacrament meeting you are hoping that there will be magnificent moments of inspiration where truth is shared in radiant and reachable language. But what do you do when they come? Do they slip from your memory as you're reaching for your car keys? One path to becoming a competent and effective speaker is to the collect wisdom and insight from others whose messages have been meaningful.

Jot down "golden niblets." Find a way to record ideas that touch your heart so they are remembered. It may be that the only thing you can do is scribble the thought on the back on the Church program. Remind yourself when your return home to discuss it, research it, and remember it. Perhaps a mention in the margin of your scriptures would be helpful if new insight came to an oft-told story. President Spencer W. Kimball counseled Church leaders, "I hope you make copious notes. I wish you would get in the habit of making notes in every meeting you attend and prepare to speak every week."[1]

Store them on your computer. If the idea is particularly helpful you may want to record it on your computer. Include any contextual information that would be helpful in the retelling. One way to make quotations easy to retrieve is to use a word processing program that allows you to search by individual words.

Make them visible. Some of the most powerful quotations, stories or ideas you'll ever use in a talk are ones you collect along your life journey. If it resonates for you, you may find it can do the same for others. Take the helpful phrases you've heard and stick them on the refrigerator door, record them in your day planner, tape them on your steering wheel, or attach them to your bathroom mirror. When you commit them to memory they are even more accessible than if noted in your journal. They become part of you and your speaking vocabulary.

Express a word of thanks. If a message has touched your heart deeply or ideas have been expressed with great insight, write the speaker and let them know of the impact they have had on you. This can be the most valuable step of all as it will help to cement the message in your memory and allow the speaker to sense that the energy they spent was worthwhile.

Note

1. *The Teachings of Spencer W. Kimball*, ed. Edward L. Kimball (1982), 522–23.

Read Widely

He shall read therein all the days of his life:
that he may learn to fear the Lord his God,
to keep all the words of this law and these statutes, to do them.

Deuteronomy 17:19

Great speakers are voracious readers. One of the reasons they are considered interesting is that they can draw on a multitude of sources to make their point. Literature, current events, history, mythology, science, poetry—they all contribute to seeing the world through a different set of eyes.

The printed word is processed differently by the mind than the spoken word. As a result, it is also stored differently. You need to read as well as listen.

If you consider general conference talks as an ideal model, you will discover a great variety of sources regarded as appropriate for a sermon. Sometimes these sources will answer questions—sometimes they will create deeper questions. As you ponder the words of others, you will make surprising connections to the important truths of the gospel. Here are just a few that may add to the research you do for your next sermon.

Newspaper. Depending on your topic, you may want to read archived historical newspapers rather than the one just tossed on your porch this morning. Newspapers are fascinating historical snapshots of your community, nation and world. You may be surprised where you find something of value—the sports page, local news, obituaries, or editorial page. Even advertisements can contribute.

Atlas. It's always better to know where a place is than to guess or, even worse, to assume incorrectly. Check what places are nearby. Learn about weather patterns, sources of water, farming practices, diseases, raw materials, and commerce. The more you know, the more confident you feel. Geography may not have been your best subject in school, but it affects every aspect of the human condition.

Great literature and drama. It is generally inappropriate to describe specific circumstances that have put someone in a difficult spiritual situation, even if there is something to be learned. But something similar has usually happened to someone in a book you've read or a play you've seen. Using fictional characters and the story to set the stage, you can easily discuss choice and accountability or how a simple change in behavior can lead to a different outcome.

Thoughtful essays. Articles in the *Ensign* and other Church publications can deepen insights and help draw out personal reflections that might otherwise be overlooked in independent study. Other Christian authors may have some valuable ideas that deserve consideration if you have sufficient time. As you think about adding any author's ideas to your talk, be aware of the needs of your listeners and don't go so deep that your audience cannot see an immediate application.

How-to books. You'll find parallels in the process of learning how to do something and how to grow spiritually. Learning a new skill can add special credibility. You may have forgotten just how difficult it is to break old habits or establish new ones. The awkward and humbling learning process of gaining a new skill can make a fabulous allegory that applies to everyone.

Encyclopedia. This can be a powerful resource for mining metaphors. Think of the possible gospel applications to these: the way the earth revolves around the sun, the layers of the skin that protect us, the courage of great explorers, methods for cleaning hard-water deposits or how volcanoes erupt. Sometimes the simplest bit of knowledge can create a new level of understanding for your listeners.

Magazines. One way to discuss a current trend is by studying it closely from the most authoritative and widely used sources. Whether it is music, fashion, entertainment or hobbies, there is a wealth of information to be gathered and used from subject-specific monthly periodicals. You may not always like what you find, but current information increases your credibility whether you are praising or criticizing a situation.

Poetry. Volumes of poetry are filled with emotive language that has the power to move the audience to be introspective. You can use poetic verse in a number of ways. You can read the actual poem or you may choose to gather words, ideas, or imagery that will enhance the way you tell an incident or situation.

Reading for knowledge is not relaxing, but it is rejuvenating. The words themselves may never be quoted, but the thoughts stirred within will lead to greater ideas. The knowledge you take with you to the pulpit will bless and influence those who hear your words. "And as all have not faith, seek ye diligently and teach one another words of wisdom; yea, seek ye out of the best books words of wisdom; seek learning, even by study and also by faith" (D&C 88:118).

Record Your Insights

Thus speaketh the Lord God of Israel, saying,
Write thee all the words that I have spoken unto thee in a book.

Jeremiah 30:2

Every day the Lord sends inspiration to understand the things of the world and gospel—fleeting glimpses of the eternal scheme. Sometimes it shows up in the way we explain things to a child. Sometimes it's a deeper understanding of a scripture. Sometimes it's a great "Aha" moment.

Put pen to paper. Or fingers to computer keys. Capture those marvelous morsels of the infinite. Perhaps your writings will be for your eyes only or maybe they will give your great-grandchildren encouragement and strength. Regardless, there is value in striving to see the hand of the Lord in your life and making a record.

The scriptures are, in large measure, the writings of great prophets who felt compelled by the Spirit to record a combination of historical, spiritual and personal events. As even the most casual reading of the scriptures will reveal, the events are not all pleasant nor do they consistently have happy endings.

Not everyone in the scriptures treasured the inspired writings left behind by previous generations. The book of Omni could easily be called "The Lost Years." Except for Amaleki, no one saw any value in adding to the plates. They seemed to see their job as protecting them and passing them on as a family heirloom. Their myopia leaves us with a spiritual question mark for those years.

Nephi took the plates seriously. And he didn't whitewash his life; he was willing to describe just how hard life can be. Following the death of his father, Lehi, Nephi saw his entire extended family crumbling into fractious disarray—a situation over which he had no control. You can feel his dark tortured emotions turning inward with harsh self-condemnation.

Nephi's lament. "O wretched man that I am! Yea, my heart sorroweth because of my flesh; my soul grieveth because of mine iniquities . . . my heart groaneth because of my sins" (2 NEPHI 4:17, 19). Yet only a few sentences later, the Spirit helps him sense his personal redemption in this trial, giving renewed hope to him and to any who identify with his plight.

Nephi's psalm. "I know in whom I have trusted. My God hath been my support; he hath led me through mine afflictions. . . . Awake, my soul! No longer droop in sin. Rejoice, O my heart, and give place no more for the enemy of my soul" (2 NEPHI 4:19, 20, 28). Without both of these, we would have less insight into the struggle Nephi faced and how he found meaning in his life and faith sufficient to meet the demands of the day.

Breaking free of the constraints of a daily record can sometimes allow the truly powerful and meaningful to emerge. Uninvited life experiences can push you to a new comprehension that would be too complex for a typical journal entry. It may be more appropriate to write an essay on a singular topic. That will urge deeper and more complex ideas to be forced to the surface. Saving your insights as a separate article will make your learning more accessible than if buried somewhere in a journal. Both your psalms and your laments deserve to be expressed and remembered.

Start with Plenty

Put ye in the sickle, for the harvest is ripe.

Joel 3:13

Inviting friends and family over to share a meal is a great way to explore unfamiliar tastes and exotic cultures. The creativity is a challenge, the aromas draw everyone to the kitchen and then you gobble up the evidence. However, the fun becomes frustration when essential ingredients are missing.

The same frustration can be felt when you begin with too little information to write a sermon. There is no worse feeling than trying to stretch a tiny undeveloped idea into a full-fledged sacrament meeting talk. It never really works, and explains why many feel uncomfortable speaking in sacrament meeting.

Start with a basketful of possibilities. Go through your personal library like a cook at the farmer's market, gathering anything that looks delicious. From this bounteous harvest you can begin selecting the brightest and best ingredients for your spiritual feast.

Gather written materials. Once you have your topic, your mission and your message, it's time to let the fun begin. Stop off at your local library. Log on to the Church Web site. Check with other ward members. Check the nearest LDS bookstore. Grab your recent copies of the *Ensign*, particularly the conference issues.

Clear a workspace. It may take more space than you think. Set up an extra table if needed. Organize the books, magazines and scriptures for easy access. Make sure it's well-lit so you don't get tired too quickly.

Clear a block of time. You'll want to have a block of time that is uninterrupted so you can keep track of the ideas as they come to you.

Seek the Holy Spirit to guide you in the sifting and selecting. Not everything you discover on your topic will be suitable for your sermon. Lean on inspiration in the selection process. Be careful of trying to force something to fit in that shouldn't be in your talk. Don't be afraid to set something aside.

Jot notes as you read. Decide if you'll be writing directly to a computer or if you'll be drafting your sermon on a tablet. Write down everything that occurs to you as you're studying so that no great ideas get lost. It's much easier to cut something out than to try to remember.

The whole process can be delightful. Never think of it as wasteful if you don't use a specific idea or resource—think of it as placing great ideas in a reservoir to be used another day. "Seek not to declare my word, but first seek to obtain my word, and then shall your tongue be loosed; then, if you desire, you shall have my Spirit and my word, yea the power of God unto the convincing of men" (D&C 11:21).

Keep a Journal

And the Lord said unto Moses,
Write this for a memorial in a book,
and rehearse it in the ears of Joshua.

Exodus 17:14

Almost everyone has them—random books and binders with disconnected personal thoughts recorded over numerous years. Can those words be of value in writing a sermon? Yes, they can. Recapturing the pain, jubilation, or complexity of a situation by memory alone is rarely enough. The words you took the time to write down can be significant resource whenever called upon to speak.

If you're not keeping a journal now, you may want to start today. Even brief notes on a moment of major significance can call to mind details that would have otherwise been forgotten. The mind is amazing—but hardly a perfect storage and retrieval system.

Speaking of which, you may want to consider keeping a computerized journal in your word processing program. It may lack some of the charm of your own handwritten version, but it is much easier to search for certain phrases or dates electronically. And you can easily make archival copies.

Your thoughts and feelings, recorded contemporaneously with important events, can be a rich resource for inspirational material. Without a written record of some kind the experience may never have significance beyond the moment it occurred. Write it down. Your memory isn't good enough to remember every spiritual experience you have had, especially if you need to call up details in order to use it in a sermon. Then, as prompted by the Holy Ghost, selectively share that which will edify.

It is certainly valuable to record the everyday happenings in your life, but make certain that you also notice and record the moments that matter in a more spiritual context. This chronological record of your sojourn will remind you and others of the challenging nature of mortality and the degree of faith required to face life's unpredictability.

Blessings. Jot down the simple blessings as well as the remarkable ones. A testimony that the Lord is mindful of the little moments in your life can be easily woven into a talk.

Gifts. When you discover a spiritual gift, mention both the gift and how the Lord used it to bless you and others. You may also notice gifts in others and realize how you've been blessed by them

Challenges. Aren't we glad that Job was willing to record the inconceivable series of tragedies, disappointments and betrayals that he suffered? One has to wonder what we would measure our trials against if Job had just set down his pen and said, "Nobody wants to read about this mess!" Write them down. Then, as the Lord reveals His holy hand in your healing, you can mention that too.

Miracles. Sometimes the intervention of the Lord is on a grand scale—and with a grand purpose. Record your experience and what it meant to you. Reviewing those entries can be consoling in times of uncertainty. When thinking about mentioning the divine manifestations in a sacrament meeting talk, we have been counseled to be highly selective in how and when these are shared. Their sacred nature demands the utmost care.

Administrations. Confirmations, ordinations, father's blessings, healings, baby blessings and being set apart for a new calling contain specific counsel and promises. Write down the phrases that stand out in your mind at the time.

Insights. Sometimes a scripture passage or story will hit you in a totally new way. Don't be afraid to jot it down as it may never strike you that way again. If someone else sends you a ray of celestial light, you may want to include that also.

Sermons. Although not easy to place in your journal, you probably want to find a way to retain a copy of your sacrament meeting talks. They can be referred to for additional insight later on. They can be a starting point for a new approach to a related topic. In your journal record how you felt about the experience as that will be an important record of your spiritual temperament for that one moment in time.

Your journal is a record of your journey. It doesn't have to be a daily document, but what you do choose to leave behind in writing often becomes one of the most valuable treasures in your estate.

Good Examples

Let thy saints rejoice in goodness.

2 Chronicles 6:41

Which one is more effective—a good example or a bad one? They both can be effective, but need to be used to point toward goodness. Just because we have the stories of Laman and Lemuel in the Book of Mormon doesn't mean we want to take our next family vacation with two boys like that. Negative examples can be powerful as members can see the consequence of a certain choice without having to experience it. When looking for narratives that help support the idea of obedience to a gospel principle, look for ones that show the classic Christian heroic struggle against evil and ultimate triumph through the Savior.

There is no expectation that the hero of the story will be sinless as that claim belongs to the Savior alone. But stories of humility, devotion, conversion and service lift us all. Use examples which show the joy of a godly life. In every case, your audience is looking for a happy ending—the happiness experienced by those who have committed their lives to the Savior. "I would desire that ye should consider on the blessed and happy state of those that keep the commandments of God" (Mosiah 2:41).

Create
A Meaningful Message

I create the fruit of the lips.

Isaiah 57:19

You Are Naturally Creative

So God created man in his own image . . .
And God blessed them, and God said unto them,
Be fruitful, and multiply, and replenish the earth, and subdue it.

Genesis 1:27–28

You were born with God-given genius within you. It may feel hidden or inaccessible at times. But it's still there. However underutilized or underdeveloped, it is there.

The reality. Every time you solve a problem, ask a question, write a letter, move an object, create a meal or hum a tune you are being creative. By changing the world around you, even subtly, you place your unique stamp on it. Remember, you are far more than a fascinating upright primate who has opposing thumbs. You are a creation of the Father. You are imaginative, resourceful, and totally original. You were created in the image of God, who is the Creator of heaven and earth. Try to feel those inborn creative powers emerging. You were born to create.

The reason. We have been commanded to *subdue* the earth and that requires creativity. Subduing our own insecurities may be the first step to unleashing our creativity. Once we do, then we can contribute in wonderful ways.

Writing a sermon for sacrament meeting is among the highest forms of creative activity. Accomplished with the right attitude, it is a totally selfless endeavor. It is not for your comfort—in fact it is often quite uncomfortable. It is not for your wealth—you will do it for free. It is not for your fame—you hope it is your *message* that will be remembered. You are doing it for others, hoping they will be blessed by your creative efforts.

The process. Some creative enterprises are more demanding than others, calling upon every mental and spiritual resource available. But you can do it. Functioning at your highest level of creativity for a sacred purpose will cause an almost electric current to run through you. You are co-creating with the Lord. In some ways, the process is more valuable than the ultimate product—at least for you.

Learning to create hybrid ideas with the raw elements of your environment is a process in itself, one which requires attention and focus. You do this by combining ideas from different sources and hybridizing your solution or response.

Nephi is a great example. He took the words of Isaiah, a prophet who preceded him by more than a century, and made certain that his family could see the immediate meaning and application of his words upon their arrival in the promised land. "I did read unto them that which was written by the prophet Isaiah; for I did liken all scriptures unto us, that it might be for our profit and learning" (1 NEPHI 19:23). What did he say? Did he see something in their new environment or condition that he could connect to the words of Isaiah?

Sermon writing can be fun as it urges us to employ the creative process. You have to find new ways of discussing familiar gospel topics. How? Introduce yourself to new people, new ideas, new processes, and new places. The scriptures may have the answers, but sometimes the creativity comes in asking new questions. Jolt yourself out of the predictable and commonplace.

To boost your creativity, find your childlike sense of wonder and pick an activity or two from this list:

Walk a new route and notice everything along the way—flowers blooming, road repairs, dogs barking, new construction, leaves in the gutter or children playing.

Listen to a different radio station for three minutes. Figure out what type of music they're playing, what they're advertising and who their audience is.

Read a columnist in the newspaper you don't normally read. Try to understand the point of view and rationale.

Learn a new word and use it five times in one day. Send an email, make a phone call, talk to a neighbor, and put it in your journal.

Buy an unfamiliar ingredient in the grocery store and find three recipes using that ingredient. Cook one of the dishes for dinner.

Write a rhyming verse for a birthday card and then send it to a friend or relative who wouldn't be expecting it.

Follow an insect for three minutes and try to figure out what life is like in their world.

Spend 30 minutes with a couple of five-year-old children and have them explain something to you. Perhaps they can tell why the sun goes down, what it's like to be an earthworm, where the wind comes from or why stars fall out of the sky.

Pick up a magazine at the doctor's office that you wouldn't normally read. Absorb words, ideas, images, processes and products from an unfamiliar world.

Design your cemetery headstone with everything except the dates. Think of how you would like your life described in a dozen words or less.

Plant a fragrant herb by your front door. Try peppermint, rosemary, chives, oregano, lemon balm or lavender. Enjoy the scent and make connections to memories from years gone by.

Now ponder the experience you've just had. It will open up new pathways in your mind and let you make new and exciting connections. Place those ideas in the context of the message you are creating for sacrament meeting. Can a barking dog represent a nagging parent? Will a fragrant herb bring to mind the scent of myrrh left behind in the empty tomb? Can the radio advertisements lead you to a come up with a new phrase to describe a gospel principle? Can a spicy hot dish give new meaning to the description of flames that are "unquenchable"?

Calling upon the creative juices flowing in your veins helps you avoid sinking into formulaic patterns and easy, quick solutions. Urge yourself uphill. You can always find a better answer or a deeper question by tapping into your heavenly gift of creativity.

A word of caution. It's more important to be effective than clever. Always measure the idea you are considering against your spiritually grounded mission statement. Your idea should support your objective, or it should not be included.

A Plain Path

Teach me thy way, O Lord, and lead me in a plain path.

Psalm 27:11

Hiking in the Rocky Mountains is so refreshing. Lace up a pair of boots and within hours you can be experiencing breathtaking vistas, challenging terrain, fields of wildflowers and the cooling spray from waterfalls. However, I admit to getting a bit anxious when I'm in unfamiliar territory. My nerves fray a little further with no map. The anxiety increases even more if no one in the group has ever hiked the area before. I have been known to stand paralyzed at a trailhead, demanding to know which path to take, notwithstanding Robert Frost's well-known advice. I just don't want to risk getting lost by starting out on the wrong path.

Likewise, one of the most daunting aspects of writing a sacrament meeting talk can be taking the first step down one path or another. The task can seem overwhelming. First of all, relax. Some of the frustration can be removed by approaching the writing process systematically. This five-step path can help you efficiently create a sermon with a clearly defined message:

1. Select your topic (or refine the one assigned to you). Define what area you intend to focus on—a gospel principle, a commandment, a moment in Church history, a scripture story, a prophet, a godly attribute, a powerful personal experience. There are limitless possibilities. Start with a broad scope and then narrow, narrow, narrow. The next step will logically follow.

2. Develop a mission statement. As you consider your audience, write down what you want to accomplish with them. They are your purpose for speaking. Prayerfully decide what you want ward members to know, do, feel or believe when you are finished speaking. Post your mission statement at the top of the page you are using to assemble your ideas. *Example:* Inspire ward members to see the hand of the Lord in both successes and setbacks.

3. Define your message. If you have a well-written talk and you deliver it well, ward members will normally take home one idea. Although that hardly seems fair, the good news is that you get to choose what that one idea is. If you can package it neatly into one concise sentence, they are more likely to remember it. Your carefully selected and organized main points. *Example:* Tithing funds are used to support the threefold mission of the Church—to preach the gospel, perfect the Saints and redeem the dead.

4. Do gospel research and find support. Nothing unravels a good talk faster than random, disconnected thoughts with no support from the scriptures or words of modern-day prophets. Spend significant time with the scriptures and you will find support for the message you want to share. Fringe benefit: Reading those related passages will clarify your thinking and open your mind to additional insights and inspiration.

5. Develop a strong introduction and conclusion. How you start and end your talk really matters. Your introduction makes them hungry for your message. Your conclusion reminds them of the great spiritual nourishment they have just received. Finally, reinforce your ideas by restating the message, which is the main concept you want them to remember.

By taking these steps, you will acquire a pattern of sermon development that results in a message with clarity and energy. You will be excited to deliver it.

Select Your Topic

Thus saith the Lord, I offer thee three things; choose thee one of them.

2 Samuel 24:12

What kind of devious person came up with the idea of an ice cream store with dozens and dozens of flavors? Not everyone thinks that is cruel, but some are unnerved by that many choices. Especially when you have to narrow your selection to just one.

Having more than a few options to choose from while selecting a sacrament meeting topic can be frustrating. Whenever possible, have the priesthood leader who invited you to speak provide you with at least a general theme. If you are left with the entire universe of gospel topics to choose from, you may find this four-step process helpful.

1. Narrow down the universe. Begin with prayer. Grab a blank piece of paper and jot down any responses that immediately come to mind as you read these questions. If you've been given a specific topic, then answer the questions within the framework of the theme given.

- ✦What challenges have I faced?
- ✦Who is a mentor for me in the scriptures?
- ✦What has strengthened my relationship with the Savior?
- ✦What adversity have I overcome?
- ✦What important lesson have I learned?
- ✦What testimony-building experiences have I had?
- ✦What scripture passages come to mind?

2. **Limit the field to three.** Look over the list you've created. You have to feel good about the variety of ideas that have surfaced. Circle the ideas or topics that stand out. Go with your immediate reaction or feelings. Work with the topics until you've narrowed the list to three.

3. **Target practice.** Your task is to narrow your selection to one by considering your listeners, your knowledge and your personal experience. Play with each of the topics. Rank them in order of preference. Then rank them in order of practicality. Which topic can you imagine yourself discussing with ward members? Do you have the resources? Time? Inclination? The Lord will guide you. You can't pick a *wrong* topic. So muster up your courage and make a selection.

4. **Conduct a feasibility study.** Before you start writing, make sure it's possible to address your chosen topic in the time you've been given. Step back and look at the topic with a clear vision of what you're attempting to tackle. The most common problem is that the topic is too broad. Don't take on too much to discuss in the few minutes allotted for a typical sacrament meeting talk. What you're looking for is more *rifle* and less *shotgun*. Once you've narrowed your topic sufficiently, you're ready to move on to the next challenge—developing a clearly defined mission for your message.

Develop a Mission Statement

They have come up hither to hear the pleasing word of God, yea, the word which healeth the wounded soul.

Jacob 2:8

As you begin preparing your sacrament meeting talk, you will need to decide what you intend to accomplish. Having a topic alone is insufficient. To assist you in developing a defined purpose, it may be helpful to think of the types of talks normally heard in sacrament meeting each Sunday.

Sacrament meeting sermons fall into three general categories, based on purpose. Typically, they will *inspire, motivate* or *explain*. You may find that you have components of all three in some talks, but there will really only be one purpose. Think carefully about this. What do you want ward members *know, do, feel* or *believe* when you are finished speaking? What does the Savior want ward members to *know, do, feel* or *believe* when you are finished speaking? If your assigned topic is "Adversity Builds Your Faith in Christ," consider how it might be presented differently but effectively in each type of sermon.

Inspire: Help listeners feel positive about a gospel principle.
Motivate: Encourage listeners to take a specific course of action.
Explain: Assist listeners to understand a principle more deeply or accurately.

Determine which category best fits the purpose of your sermon. Draft a statement that explains the mission for your message.

Examples of Mission Statements

Inspire: Lift the hearts of ward members facing adversity by helping them see the hand of the Lord in their trials.
Motivate: Encourage ward members faced with adversity to fast for understanding, develop patience and fortify their relationship with the Savior.
Explain: Help ward members to see that adversity strengthens their faith in Christ.

The more specific your mission statement, the more quickly you'll find support materials. Place that statement in bold letters and in plain sight at the top of the sheet you're using to collect your information and ideas. It will then be easier to select support materials to help you achieve your objective. In fact, you will find that as soon as you have developed your mission, information will begin flowing to you. Your mission will also provide maximum motivation to finalize the content and rehearse the delivery so that when you complete your talk you can say, "Mission accomplished."

Define Your Message

Remember, remember that it is upon the rock of our Redeemer, who is Christ, the Son of God, that ye must build your foundation.

Helaman 5:12

A classic scene in movie and television scripts has a quarreling couple going back and forth until one of them stops suddenly and says, "Exactly what is your point?" With a startled look the other replies, "I can't remember, but I'm sure it was important."

How does something that seemed so important in the beginning get lost by the end of the conversation? Simple—the point did not remain the focus. This won't happen to your sacrament meeting talk if you decide specifically, in advance, what it is you want your listeners to remember.

As you ponder that take-home message, draft a single compact sentence that you want listeners to remember when you are finished speaking. The more specific your sentence, the more likely you are to craft a sermon that will make it easy for ward members to recall it. Place it in plain sight, near your mission statement. Those two sentences define what you want to accomplish by the time you sit down. Make it so that members of the ward remember more than your topic—you want them to remember the fresh insights and the positive applications you discussed.

Your message statement needs to remain somewhat fluid during the initial stages of sermon creation. This allows for modification based on either new information or spiritual guidance. As you continue to research and write it will begin to solidify.

It's tempting to skip these steps assuming that if your motives are pure, somehow a mission and message will evolve and be accomplished. It's not very likely and not really fair to your listeners.

Example of a Message: Adversity can be made meaningful through fasting, patience and growing closer to Christ.

Take the time to define your main message and long after the "Amens" have evaporated, your message will stick to memory.

Use Scriptures Accurately

If ye suppose that ye cannot worship God,
ye do greatly err, and ye ought to search the scriptures;
if ye suppose that they have taught you this,
ye do not understand them.

Alma 33:2

One crisp autumn morning, while driving through the Alps on my way through Switzerland, I came upon a small sign that read, *Sustenpass geschlossen*. I figured it meant, "Sustenpass straight ahead." If you speak German you are already laughing; if you don't you'll be laughing soon. As I zoomed straight up into the mountains, the windy road took me past beautiful forests, waterfalls, and then suddenly—a giant wall of snow! *Geschlossen* means closed! That explains why there were no other cars on the road. I tried to guess the meaning of the sign, and I was wrong. We can easily make the same mistake by misreading a word or two in the scriptures.

Let's take a look at a frequently misunderstood scripture passage in the New Testament. "Search the scriptures; for in them ye think ye have eternal life: and they are they which testify of me" (John 5:39). What seems at first to be a suggestion to study the scriptures, upon further examination is found to be a stinging chastisement by the Savior. As you study the fifth chapter of John with all the footnotes, the meaning of the passage becomes clear.

To whom was the Savior speaking? Jewish leaders who were so angry with Him they wanted Him to be killed.

Following what event? The Savior healing the man at the pool of Bethesda.

Why were the Jews angry? He healed a man on the Sabbath.

Is that all? They were even angrier when He declared that His power to do so came from the Father.

What did the Savior say in His defense? He proclaimed His divine sonship.

What was the reaction? He was condemned as a blasphemer.

How did the Savior try to establish His sacred role in their eyes? The Law of Witnesses, using their acknowledged veneration for John the Baptist and Moses.

What was the final condemnation spoken by the Savior? "Search the scriptures; for in them ye *think* ye have eternal life: and they are they which testify of *me*" [italics added for emphasis] (JOHN 5:39).

It's easy to take a passage "out of context" and miss the powerful original intent. Before citing a scripture, try to understand what is being said. Read a good portion of scripture that precedes it. Find out what follows. Read historical notes. Check cross-references. Come to know the author. Consider the original audience for whom it was intended. Imagine the day it was first written down or spoken. Lead your listeners to the words, author and application.

Lead to the words. As you determine how a particular passage can support the point you are making in your talk, avoid the temptation to simply drop it into your talk. Instead, consider how the members need to be lead to the words. Identify the key words or phrases and make sure they stand out.

Lead to the author. Sharing contextual information helps the audience to gain a love and appreciation for the person you will be quoting. The more you know of who spoke or wrote the words, the more you will care. Including the details of the events leading up to that moment can also add to the impact.

Lead to the application. Giving further insights as to the application of the counsel allows the audience to become hungry for the information. Blessings, inspiration, protection and guidance are examples of desirable outcomes that can come from specific applications of the counsel found in the scriptures. "With all thy getting get understanding" (PROVERBS 4:7).

SPEAK PLAINLY

I had rather speak five words with my understanding
that by my voice I might teach others also,
than ten thousand words in an unknown tongue.

1 CORINTHIANS 14:19

PAUL HAD IT RIGHT—better to speak a few words that are understood than volumes that no one understands. It's easy to get entangled in a model that causes you to think the bigger the word the better. In sacrament meeting, the clarity of a simple well-chosen word will always be more effective than unfamiliar multi-syllabic vocabulary. This is where sensitivity to your listeners is essential.

The old saw from journalism may be helpful here: Never overestimate the knowledge of your audience, but never underestimate their intelligence. In other words, don't talk over their heads and don't talk down to them. This is a delicate balance to be sure—but one that can be managed when a conversational tone is established.

Choose ideas and words that are well-suited to your ward. Your purpose is not to impress, but to inspire. Complicated, academic and heavily adorned language can be a stumbling block to communication rather than a bridge. Plain talk, plain ideas, plain truth and plain testimony are easily and widely understood.

Plain talk. Use the simplest words that will communicate your thoughts. Avoid using words that aren't normally in your vocabulary, as you may stumble over them or misuse them.

Plain ideas. Create a message that can be followed by all. Straightforward, uncomplicated ideas that are creatively presented will often leave the longest impression.

Plain truth. Make the eternal truths of the gospel plain and accessible to every one who listens.

Plain testimony. Fortify your message with a clear testimony of the principle you have just taught.

The result of striving to be easily understood, is a message that will be taken and remembered. The Holy Ghost will testify that your message is true. "For my soul delighteth in plainness; for after this manner doth the Lord God work among the children of men" (2 NEPHI 31:3).

Make Quotes Stand Out

And say thou unto them, Thus saith the Lord.

Jeremiah 11:3

To increase the vitality of your message, especially the individual main points, use the thoughts and ideas of Church leaders and other notable thinkers. A quote should represent a clear, concise and powerful thought—one that will generate a desire to do good. You can quote directly or paraphrase in order to convey the information. These guidelines can apply to scripture passages as well as quotes from other sources.

How to select quotes. The process of selecting a quote for a talk is a lot like selecting produce in the market. When you need something fresh and delicious to serve your family you may wander up and down the rows of produce, hefting an orange or two, sniffing the pineapples and testing the apples for firmness. You want to select the best. That means you can't run into the store and grab the first fruit that you see. The selection process must be thoughtful and deliberate.

Study a wide array of resources, so that the quote selected will be the most supportive of the point you're trying to make.

Consider the credibility of the source—current counsel from prophets will always be the most powerful, but wisely chosen advice from others can also be valid and supportive.

Go to your own favorite sources and find the insights and ideas you have collected that have special meaning to you.

Once selected, search for deeper understanding of the quote by studying the speaker, historical context, conflict, situation and meaning, as well as cultural and religious impact.

Sometimes a negative quote from a clearly evil source can set the stage for a spiritual solution. Use a quote like this carefully and with a clear purpose.

Best sources for quotes are biographies, great literature and plays, letters of influential historical figures, historically significant speeches, current events and books of religious writings.

How to use quotes in your talk. Once the best are selected, how you use your quotes is like serving your carefully selected fruit. You don't just roll the apples on to the table and assume your family will enjoy them. You clean them, peel them, slice them and present them in an appealing manner.

Give listeners a reason to be *hungry* for the quote that you will you share. Tap into the questions and concerns of the congregation.

Mention a predicament or problem to which you have a noteworthy solution.

Bring up the actual situation that precipitated the quote, allowing listeners to see the process that generated the insight.

Point out the unique credentials or experience of the person and why you should take the advice of this person seriously. It's especially helpful to find connections and common ground.

Tell the story of how you came across this particular idea and what impact it had on your life.

Prune the text of the quote to the very essence of the message, selecting the fewest words with the greatest meaning. Don't be afraid to cut unnecessary phrases, as long as you do not change the meaning and intent of the original passage.

Rehearse it sufficiently so that you can read it smoothly, expressively and with maximum confidence and eye contact. Double-check the pronunciation of any unfamiliar words.

Since speaking is an auditory experience, be sure to give attribution before you give the quote or paraphrase so listeners will be appropriately prepared to receive the message.

Make certain that you understand what the quote really means. This may include looking up words in the dictionary.

If you introduce the quote well and pause briefly at the conclusion, there is no need to say "quote" at the beginning or "unquote" at the end. Practice so that the quote stands out.

Avoid introducing a quote by saying "Here's a quote on . . . " or "I will now read to you . . . " Find an intriguing way to draw the audience in.

Be especially careful of rushing a quote. To give a quotation more gravity and importance, lower your voice slightly and speak deliberately. Make certain your voice goes down in pitch at the end to signify the conclusion of the quote. But do not let your voice trail off in volume. Stay strong to the end.

Just as delicious and carefully chosen fruits can enhance a meal, well-selected quotes delivered expressively can enhance your message. Quotes can emphasize a particular point and make it memorable.

Take Notes

And now I, Mormon,
make a record of the things
which I have both seen and heard.

Mormon 1:1

Making a decision on your topic is one of the most important steps you take in the sermon-writing process. Once you commit to a topic, information will begin flowing to you from every direction. It's the change in focus that makes it happen.

Try this experiment. Look around the room and identify every item that is red. Red almost leaps off the shelves. You see it in every nook and cranny. It's woven into every piece of fabric and splashed on every magazine cover. Where did it all come from? It was always there, but when your attention was redirected, you noticed it.

As you become sensitized to your topic, you will hear speakers talk about it, you will see articles in the paper that relate to it, you will start seeing connections to unrelated topics. Be prepared to capture insights as they appear. Ideas come out of nowhere. But when it's time to start writing, it's sometimes difficult to get the ideas flowing.

A simple tool—the 3″ x 5″ card—can give you a way to record ideas as they come to you and keep you from ever saying, "Now, what was that great idea I had yesterday?"

Keep a card at your bedside. Great ideas often come right after prayer or when you first wake up in the morning. Even waiting a few minutes can cause a sparkling insight to disappear.

Keep a card in your wallet. When you're standing in line at the grocery store or the bank, your mind can wander. You may see a situation that you can use to illustrate a principle.

Keep a card in your glove box. How people treat each other at the gas station, while waiting to turn left, when changing lanes, or even in the parking lot can reveal much of the human condition. Jot down the details and make it into a story.

Keep a card by your computer. While surfing the net, you bump into a lot of information and loads of current events. Some is totally useless, but some is brilliant. If there is something usable, don't print out the whole article; shrink it down to a usable size.

Keep a card in your scriptures. As you read, you will come across passages that will surprise you with new and deeper meaning. Write down the insight and key words. Add cross-references and any other resources.

SEEING IS BELIEVING

I believed not the words, until I came,
and mine eyes had seen it.

1 KINGS 10:7

ALTHOUGH IT MAY SEEM ODD, visual aids can be effectively used to enhance a sermon in sacrament meeting. Some visual aids are part of every presentation, others are add-ons that must be carefully selected. But just as we are counseled regarding meat in the Word of Wisdom, visual aids should be used sparingly.

You. Keep in mind that you are the first visual component listeners will notice. Dress to show reverence and to be taken seriously.

Scriptures. Always bring a set of scriptures to the pulpit as you will want to quote from them. They are your most valuable visual aid, evidence that you are using the Word of God. Leave other books behind as quotes from those sources can be written into your notes.

Text. Bring your well-prepared notes to the pulpit, even if you could give the sermon without them. It shows conscientious preparation and that you are not trying to "wing it."

Evidence. When telling a dramatic story that is the centerpiece of your sermon, sometimes there is an item that can be pulled out at just the right moment to underscore the significance. If you were telling of a time that you were preserved in a near-fatal automobile accident, the smashed side mirror held up briefly could add a feeling of realism. Avoid photos or any item that is too small or complex to be identified immediately. Although it wasn't in a Church meeting, Captain Moroni certainly understood the value of a visual aid. He went forth among the people, "waving the rent part of his garment in the air, that all might see the writing which he had written" (Alma 46:19).

Metaphor. This calls upon your deepest creativity as you work through your talk. If you find a metaphor that will work and the object can be identified from the pulpit, you may want to use it. President Boyd K. Packer is well-known for his famous glove-and-hand story regarding the separation of body and spirit at death.[1] A clock, a piece of fruit, a set of keys, a boomerang—there are many items that can be appropriately used.

Reminder. A piece of history, such as a baby bonnet worn on the day your grandmother was blessed or the missionary journal of an ancestor, can be a tender connection to the past. This could be an effective way to show that family history is more than just names—it's appreciating the lives of those who have gone before.

Although we live in a visual culture, where seeing is believing, be highly selective in anything that you bring as a visual aid. They can be effective in making a message more memorable, but have the potential of being distractive rather than supportive. You may want to check with your priesthood leader if you have any doubts.

Note

1. "Behold Your Little Ones," *Ensign*, July 1973, 51.

Engage the Senses

All thy garments smell of myrrh, and aloes, and cassia.

Psalm 45:8

Finding illustrations, examples, narratives or stories is like a treasure hunt. It's always exciting to find just the right one. But you should enjoy the search also. Once found, develop the story to fit into your talk effortlessly. As you tell stories, be sure to include details that engage all five senses. This helps the story come alive.

Sight. Use details that emphasize colors, designs, shapes, unusual characteristics. Our visual memories may be unreliable, but we can recreate them with a speaker as a story is told. *Example:* "Although the little girl's blue gingham dress was wrinkled and stained and her feet were bare, she approached the missionaries . . ."

Smell. Use details that bring back scents linked with specific memories, events, or incidents. Gasoline, perfume, old tennis shoes, the cat's litter box—anything with a distinct smell should be mentioned. *Example:* "As I opened the door, the entire house was filled with the comforting aroma of mom's pumpkin pie . . . "

Hearing. Make the sounds help draw the picture. Almost any story has sounds connected to it—some may be startling, others soothing. Each sound adds a level of depth to the story. *Example:* "I heard the unmistakable crash and tinkle of breaking glass as my baseball flew through the window of the ward building . . . "

Taste. Even though tastes are difficult to describe, there are certain flavors and tastes that everyone knows. Tap into the common ground of cultural habits to add taste when it's possible. *Example:* "My mouth puckered as I sensed that the lemonade was just a little short on sugar . . . "

Touch. Explore sensations of touch—rough/smooth, hot/cold, painful/soothing, wet/dry. It makes the listener remember the same feelings and identify with the person who is having the experience. *Example:* "As she slipped into the snug hand-made Christmas sweater, she didn't have the heart to tell her grandmother how scratchy is was against her skin . . . "

Now as valuable as these strategies may be, there are two other issues that you'll need to think about while weaving the story into your text:

Write succinctly. Use as few words as possible to convey the details of the story. Set the stage well but sparsely.

Stop. Know when to finish the story. There is always something more to be told, but you need to predetermine the concluding elements so you can make your point.

ANCHOR SERMONS IN CHRIST

What manner of man is this,
that even the wind and the sea obey him?

MARK 4:41

THOSE WHO HAVE BEEN ABOARD a sailing ship in a storm understand the value of an anchor—a solid, heavy, dependable, immovable anchor. The ocean, a powerful surging mass of salt water, can easily overcome any vessel that dares to cross her. Understandably, a tradition of praying for sailors and seaman exists in almost every culture with a coastline. Venturing on to the sea with only a wooden hull and fabric sails as protection has always been an adventure in faith.

Ships are especially vulnerable to changes in the weather and must have a method to keep from being dashed to pieces on coastal rocks or unexpected shallows. The only method to secure a ship during a storm is an anchor. To *drop anchor* means to lower a massive weight connected to the ship by a heavy chain. To keep the ship in a safe position the anchor must be submerged and securely planted on the seabed below.

Likewise, Christ is our anchor in the storms of life. And just like seamen of old, we need to know how to get into a safe position by using this sacred anchor in our lives. Christ then becomes the anchor of every message.

No matter the topic, the principle, or the moment in Church history that you are discussing, all messages, just like lives, need to be anchored in Christ. Speak in a way that shows Christ is your anchor.

Create a Sense of Urgency

Behold, I come quickly.

Revelation 3:11

One of the biggest challenges in a sermon is to move listeners from a sense of significance to a sense of urgency. Everyone is willing to acknowledge the importance of a course of action, but that alone does not move listeners to action. Your mission statement should be a reminder of what you are attempting to accomplish. Your task is not complete until you have ward members silently agreeing to your course of action.

I'm reminded of a fable I was told years ago about Satan and his minions while in a strategy session. They were greatly concerned about the progress of the kingdom of God. One of his demons suggested, "I'll go down and just tell them that none of it's true."

Satan replied, "That'll never work. These Latter-day Saints are too faithful for that bold of a lie."

Another proposed, "I'll just tell them it's only half-true to confuse them."

Satan replied, "That'll never work. Latter-day Saints study the gospel and know what they believe."

There was understandable frustration in the realms of darkness until one little demon piped up. "I know—I'll tell them it's all true . . . there's just no hurry."

Creating a sense of urgency is a gift, but a gift that can be nurtured and developed. Perhaps one of the best at this was President Spencer W. Kimball. He projected both importance and urgency in his well-remembered challenges and chastisements in the 1970s. Suddenly Saints all over the globe were planting a garden, cleaning up their yards, keeping a journal, reading the scriptures and learning to speak Chinese.

The key is to use language that underscores both the importance of the task and the risks of any delay. This will be an essential component of your conclusion. Without sounding alarmist, move ward members to take prompt action. As the favorite hymn reminds,

For promptness bringeth safety,
And blessings rich and pure.[1]

Note

1. "Improve the Shining Moments," *Hymns* (1985), no. 226.

Become a Guide

Understandest thou what thou readest?
And he said, How can I, except some man should guide me?

Acts 8:30–31

Standing in admiration, you crane your neck at an uncomfortable angle to view the massive stained glass windows in the 800-year-old Chartres Cathedral. You can't help but wonder how artisans found the commitment to sustain them as they devoted their lives to creating glass masterpieces that would be seen by relatively few. A simple unattended walk through the cathedral will leave you gasping in awe, yet you may very well miss the whole reason the windows even exist.

Malcolm Miller, an historian who has devoted his life to understanding the messages of the windows at Chartres, sees far more than lovely religious artifacts or beautiful pieces of ancient art. By guiding you from window to window, he helps visitors see 13th-century Christian theology and compares it to the beliefs of today.

It would be easy to just admire the beautiful windows as you walk past them. Instead, many are enlightened by an inspired and knowledgeable guide.

As a speaker in sacrament meeting, you can do the same for your audience. Show them what you found by studying a single verse or two in depth. By clarifying meanings of single words or phrases, you make it possible for others to remember the insights you shared every time they "walk" past that verse.

Multiple meanings. Many scriptural passages have several meanings or layers. When we search for the one true meaning, we may miss another meaning that can be equally valid and important. Explore them all, placing them in historical or cultural context. Contemplate what the original author may have been trying to say. Reading the footnotes and cross references can be helpful.

Archaic meanings. Some words, especially in the Old Testament, have fallen completely out of common usage. It may take some research to unearth the original meanings. How many times have we heard the phrase "reproving *betimes* with sharpness" (D&C 121:43), thinking that "betimes" means "at times" or "occasionally?" In Joseph Smith's day, "betimes" meant "instantly," or "in a timely manner."

Obscured meanings. The meaning of some words have been obscured over time, especially by inaccurate interpretation. Check the original Hebrew or Greek word for a more complete understanding. We read that Matthew was a "publican" (MATTHEW 10:3). A glance at the footnote shows a more understandable translation from the Greek to be "tax collector."

Unfamiliar meanings. Some words are just plain unfamiliar and deserve to be understood rather than simply skipped over. Even text from the 1830s can be easily misunderstood. Many assume that "traveling without purse or *scrip*" is like going on vacation without a checkbook or credit card. By referring to the footnote in the scriptures they are surprised to find that "scrip" is actually a traveling bag.

Check this list for words and phrases that could use some clarification.

Anon
The field is *white*, already to harvest

Enter ye in at the *strait* gate
Mote and *beam*
Kick against the *pricks*
Straitway
Manger
Mite
Farthing
Furlong
Stiffneckedness

As you speak, become a valued guide in exploring the richness contained in the word of God.

Words Have Meaning

Every idle word that men shall speak,
they shall give account thereof in the day of judgment.
For by thy words thou shalt be justified,
and by thy words thou shalt be condemned.

Matthew 12:36–37

"A set." Alone, the word has no meaning at all. In context, it can have dozens of meanings. A hair style. China dishes. What you win in tennis. Stage scenery. A collection of musical pieces. Repetitions in an exercise routine. A young plant ready to be transplanted.

Every word has at least one meaning. Most words have multiple meanings. Add to that, words have layers of sub-meaning and connotation that shade the impact. Current slang usage can take a commonly used word and turn it into something else completely. This is why dictionaries have to be republished every year. English is a dynamic language and meaning is a moving target. Sometimes it's almost scary to try to select the right word.

Being sufficiently prepared to speak means never stepping up to the podium, inside or outside the Church, without knowing the meaning of every word you intend to speak. Don't assume you know. If you have any doubt, look it up. Once it comes out of your mouth, you own it. That can be painful if you bungle it. Do your vocabulary homework in advance and you can avoid wishing for a verbal vacuum cleaner.

My most embarrassing moment with miscalculating the meaning of a word was in high school. My best friend was the high school yearbook editor and I was her assistant. We spent an entire year holed up in yearbook room cropping pictures, writing captions, making headlines, adding illustrations, writing poetry, and eating mustard burgers. It was a season of delightful memories. The last week before the yearbook went to press, we each selected a special quote to be attached to each other's senior picture—a quote that was supposed to represent an inside look at that individual.

Ginny chose for me an adaptation of quote from Alexander Pope: "I will always have something to do, someone to love and something to hope for." I, on the other hand, in a moment of ultimate editorial stupidity went for something that sounded playful, but really wasn't. "What's an ounce of mischief in an ocean of happiness?" I was sixteen and hadn't bothered to consider what the word mischief meant. To me it sounded like the quality of being lighthearted and spontaneous. But this word has serious baggage—destructive and malevolent undertones that simply escaped me at the time. When the yearbook was published, I expected her to be delighted. She was devastated.

It was a valuable lesson to learn early in life. Words have meaning. Words have power. If you have any uncertainty about the meaning of a word, double check. If the word has connotations that could color the message you're trying to give, look for another.

Choose the Best Words

Therefore shall ye lay up these my words
in your heart and in your soul.

Deuteronomy 11:18

Imagine that you've been studying English as a second language and you're finally ready to try it out. It's your first day and someone newsworthy has died. Newspaper headlines might say anything from "expired" to "slipped away in the night" to "succumbed" to "returned home." There are dozens of ways to say that someone has passed away. English has more words than any other language on earth, and therefore more choices whenever an attempt is made to put together a meaningful sentence.

Choices can be exciting, but choices can also be frustrating. The best plan is to relax and have fun with your own language. Most of us maintain a fairly limited vocabulary. Giving a talk in sacrament meeting is a good time to polish up your skills without trying to verbally intimidate your ward.

Elder Neal A. Maxwell became recognized for his ability to select not only a suitable word, but the best word, in almost every circumstance. He was a joy to listen to and learn from. As with any talent, Elder Maxwell developed it over time. Although he is no longer among us, his memory lives on as his elegant and beautifully phrased ideas are quoted frequently.

As you work on the final version of your talk, keep a dictionary and thesaurus close at hand. This is helpful whether you are planning a manuscript delivery, which demands a full-text version, or extemporaneous delivery, which needs only an outline. Some suggestions on word selection:

Be specific: Use words that create clarity; avoid vague, unclear or fuzzy words. *Example:* "Scarlet and gold brocade" is better than "red cloth." Eliminate *kinda, sorta* and *very* as they do little to increase understanding.

Be descriptive: Find adjectives and adverbs that make your examples and stories come alive, engaging all the senses. *Examples:* "painfully pungent," "dark and slippery," or "needle-like prickles."

Be emotive: Use words that bring human emotions to the surface, while keeping your emotions in check. *Example:* "She hung her head out the window of the train as she waved her final goodbye."

Be appropriate: Replace any slang with a more suitable term.

Be economical: Use the fewest words possible to get your point across; double-check for rambling stories or examples.

Be unifying: Find words that draw ward members together and create a sense of unity; eliminate divisive words.

Be reverent: Show your love for the Savior in how you mention His name, His Church and His gospel.

Word selection is best done in advance. It's crucial in the telling of a centerpiece story, as the exact word you need may not easily bubble up to the surface when you need it. Better to select the words in advance and rehearse until the text flows naturally.

Quote the Word of God

All scripture is given by inspiration of God, and is profitable for doctrine, for reproof, for correction, for instruction in righteousness.

2 Timothy 3:16

The divinely inspired words found in the holy scriptures belong in every talk given in sacrament meeting. It's the Lord's day, the Lord's meeting, the Lord's house, and the Lord's supper—it is only natural that the word of the Lord be heard in abundance. But are there ways to make those passages stand out and sink deeply into the heart?

Prune the scripture. Don't feel compelled to use every single word in a scripture passage. You can overlook the introductory words or even start halfway in. You can stop before the verse is over. Or even skip over a middle portion. Don't alter the meaning of the scripture (study it carefully, so you can be certain you understand it), but you can trim it to a manageable size for the purpose of your talk.

Make listeners hungry for the message. Give listeners a reason to care before launching into a scripture. There are lots of possibilities. Mention that you found something remarkable in the scriptures that you think will influence how ward members will consider this issue from that day forward. Or perhaps you've discovered a new insight that connects two previously disconnected events.

Read it directly from your scriptures. Even if the scripture is memorized (which actually is a pretty good idea), open the scriptures and hold them up as you briefly glance down to share the revealed word of God. As ubiquitous as PDAs are becoming, avoid citing passages from an electronic device. There is a real risk of electronic malfunction which can disrupt an otherwise great sermon. Besides, there is something beautiful about a leather-bound set of scriptures draped over the hand of the speaker.

Give it context. Answering the questions of who, what, when, where, and why gives listeners some idea of what was going on when this heavenly idea was put on to paper or scratched into metal plates. This can be a tough task. If it was important enough to write it down, listeners deserve to know a bit of background when available.

Read it expressively. This is a test of your dramatic reading skills, but it's not anything that you can't do. It takes practice. Scriptures deserve to be read with warmth and a touch of drama. Slow down and imagine the lines being delivered by an accomplished actor. The stories are so rich—birth, death, sacrifice, betrayal, testimony, temptation, redemption, consecration, martyrdom—they demand an appropriately expressive reading from the pulpit. Help others to sense the beauty and majesty of the words and the author.

Emphasize key words. Give a little *umph* to the words you want to have stand out—slow down, speak up, and wrap your voice around them. Practice carefully until you feel you will achieve the desired result. Determine in advance what words you want to emphasize and make a notation on the scripture.

Lead them to the message. Your audience needs to know what you see in the passage, not what page it is on. Reciting chapter and verse often breaks up the flow of your ideas. If you introduce it well, they will know what is happening and to whom. The scriptural reference is like a GPS—a locator system to help find the exact place in a lengthy passage. If someone is really curious, after the meeting they may ask you where the scripture can be found. You should have the reference ready to cite.

Bear your testimony of it. After reading the words, bear brief testimony that you know the message is true. The truth of the words will be multiplied by your witness.

Words from the scriptures in their honesty and purity can have a life-changing effect. All you have to do is consider the First Vision to realize what a ponderous reading of James 1:5 did for one young man in the spring of 1820. The Prophet Joseph recalled, "Never did any passage of scripture come with more power to the heart of man than this did at this time to mine. It seemed to enter with great force into every feeling of my heart. I reflected on it again and again" (JS—H 1:12).

Use Scriptures Effectively

I will shew thee that which is noted in the scripture of truth.

Daniel 10:21

There is something marvelous about having "the scriptures laid open to our understandings" (JS—H 1:74). Part of the impact of hearing scripture passages read aloud is the sound of ancient words in timeless and beloved sentences. Foreign and yet totally familiar.

But there is also something distinctively beautiful about a bound book of scriptures as they are raised up to be read. The drape of the pages and the suppleness of the binding nestled in the hand radiate antiquity and value. Even the crinkle of the turning page is wonderfully distinct and unmistakable.

Here are some keys to using your scriptures for maximum ease and effect when at the pulpit.

1. Before standing, unzip and remove your scriptures from any cover; make certain any loose pages or inserts are removed so they don't fall out when you open the scriptures.
2. When approaching the pulpit, lay your closed scriptures to one side.
3. Make sure the print is large enough to easily read from the pulpit.

4. Use sticky notes as bookmarks, so you can open right to the selected passage.
5. Write the actual scripture reference on the part that sticks out from the page; allow only a small edge of sticky note to extend beyond the page.
6. Also write a key word on the sticky note to match up to your speaker's outline.
7. Mark the scripture passage in colored pencil so that you can find it quickly on the page.
8. If you will not be using the entire passage you have colored, mark where to begin and end with small sticky notes.
9. Rehearse the passage so well that you only need to glance down to recite it.
10. Consider holding your scriptures up from the pulpit for added visual impact.
11. If you need reading glasses, have them ready.
12. Read the passage with an expressive voice, emphasizing key words.

Say More about Less

Thou shalt prune thy vineyard,
and gather in the fruit thereof.

Leviticus 25:3

I love to run in the morning and much of my route includes the hills surrounding my home. One of my neighbors has a beautiful apricot tree that he allows me to pick from each summer. Each summer that it bears fruit, that is. Nasty late spring freezes have snatched the apricot crop two years in a row. But this year was set to be a bumper crop.

Gene is a fabulous steward of his fruit trees and I fully expected that he would be out thinning the fruit to maximize the fruit size. But as spring turned into summer and the fruit began to mature, I realized that this year, due to the choices of the owner, there would be pounds and pounds of delicious, but puny fruit. The unthinned fruit pushed against each other hoping for nutrition, moisture, sunlight and space to grow. There simply wasn't enough to go around. As a result, the yield was walnut-sized apricots, which were more pit than fruit.

It is easy to fall into the trap of doing the same thing in writing sacrament meeting talks. In saying very little about a lot of different things, you may be giving more pit than fruit.

Thin early for best results. Far more effective is to do your pruning and thinning early on in the process. Select a few strong main points and develop them fully. You rarely need more than five main points. If you see you have more—start your thinning. Leave only the best points for full development. Create a big, luscious, meaty harvest for all to enjoy. You will feel better and ward members will remember more.

Your Stories Are Valuable

For I have given you an example,
that ye should do as I have done to you.

John 13:15

Using illustrations and examples from your own experience is powerful and revealing. The struggle against the adversary is real and can be appropriately addressed without revealing soul-crushing sins to the entire ward. You do not need to show you are perfect; you need to show that the pathway to the Savior is illuminated one step at a time while describing an experience on your journey.

So how do you determine if a personal story is appropriate for sacrament meeting? Here are three criteria that can help in the decision process.

The story is true. Make sure that what you're sharing really happened. Gather up the details you remember and write them down. Get your facts straight. If you were unconscious as the surgeon operated on you and the family declared the operation a miracle, check with the surgeon and others to get additional details. Don't give listeners any reason to doubt or misconstrue.

The story inspires others to do good and be better. Check the story for its core message. Does it encourage better behavior? Does it move listeners to be more generous, more kind, more faithful? Make certain that the conclusion leads listeners to making better choices.

The story illustrates a point. Make sure that the story you're using actually supports the point you're trying to make. Measure it against the standard you created with the creation of your mission statement. If it doesn't really work, save the story for another time. Don't force-fit the story into your talk.

When in doubt, throw it out. Some stories are for personal journals only. Or they may be appropriate for a family gathering where all extenuating experiences and personalities are well known. Avoid stories that describe sinful behavior, mock others, or question gospel teachings. Likewise avoid stories that simply flaunt a brush with celebrity or a privileged lifestyle. Treat any questionable story like spoiled food in the back of the refrigerator: "When in doubt, throw it out."

Personal stories can be some of the most compelling and rich to use. Be selective and develop the story for maximum impact.

Speaking in Parables

He spake a parable unto them.

Luke 6:39

One way to explain a complex intangible idea is to create a parable. What exactly is a parable? It's a literary method of explaining an unknown (or something less understood) by comparing it to something widely understood by your listeners. While that may sound complex, the process is easy.

President Boyd K. Packer shared a story in general conference containing a parable that has been retold for three decades. He recounted a visit to Africa where he was taken to see some animals in the wild. When he asked why the antelopes were afraid to approach the tiny puddles of water created by elephant tracks, the guide responded, "Crocodiles." President Packer challenged the guide, sure that no crocodile could fit in an elephant track. Upon closer examination, he saw the leathery back of a hungry crocodile, ready for an antelope breakfast. He compared the experience to youth doubting the loving guidance of parents and Church leaders. His parable taught the dangers that await those who ignore the guides we have on our life's safari.[1]

The Savior used everyday objects, processes and tasks to explain our relationship with God and our role in his kingdom. Using sheep, vines, bread, water, farming, weather and banking the Savior drew parallels that people who were "willing to hear" could understand. Look around you right now—there are dozens of objects, processes and tasks that would lend themselves to a homemade parable.

Of course, that isn't where you begin. The first step is to think about what you're trying to communicate, the point you're trying to make. Once that's clear in your mind, find an object, process or task that could shed new light on that topic. Try to develop a parable for each of these topics:

- Becoming truly converted
- Teaching the gospel
- Being an example of faithfulness
- Baptism
- Missionary work
- Doing more than is expected
- Helping someone who is struggling with their testimony

The Savior has addressed all of these with metaphorical language—the parables that match the items on the above list probably come to mind quickly. If not, look them up and see how the Savior used a parable. With a little effort, you could likely find a different object, process or task for each topic that would be common to listeners today. If you're feeling like your brain is frozen, the list below may give you some ideas. Most of the items listed did not exist at the time of the Savior.

Room. If you glance around right where you're seated you might see a light bulb, broken pencil, clock, computer, telephone, photo album, diploma, sticky note or newspaper. Which of these could be made into a parable?

Refrigerator. Digging around in the coldest place in the house, you may find milk, eggs, mustard, onions, ice cream, lettuce, potatoes, leftovers, ice cubes, maybe even a little mold. Which of these could be made into a parable?

Garage. Take a look around in that dusty garage and you're likely to notice a car, gasoline, lawn mower, power drill, hammer, rake, insecticide, cobwebs, trash can, flat tire or Christmas lights. Which of these could be made into a parable?

Outdoors. Walk out on to your front porch and breathe in the beauty of the outdoors. A few steps away you may notice ivy, dandelions, vegetable garden, fence, driveway, rain, sidewalk, clouds, caterpillars, wind or a falling star. Which of these could be made into a parable?

Library. One of the best places to start a parable search is in a "visual dictionary," a book that contains labeled illustrations of just about everything in the universe. As you ponder a combustion engine, human heart, sailing ship, microwave oven or space shuttle you can't help but think of connections to the spiritual realm. Which of these could be made into a parable?

Although developing parables can be a fun and creative process, they do have their limitations. Be careful not to carry them too far. Reach for a parable whenever you think you can use one to teach a principle more profoundly. "Why speakest thou unto them in parables? He answered and said unto them, Because it is given unto you to know the mysteries of the kingdom of heaven" (MATTHEW 13:10–11).

Note

1. "Spiritual Crocodiles," *Ensign*, May 1976, 30.

Effective Storytelling

We returned, those of us that were spared,
to the land of Zarahemla,
to relate that tale to their wives and their children.

Mosiah 9:2

Let me tell you a story. I was only five years old when my kindergarten playmate, Janine, invited me to attend weekday Primary with her. I would reverently fold my arms as I entered the unfamiliar big white chapel on Garey Avenue. I would slide across the polished wooden pews and sing Primary songs with the other children. Sister Bemis was always there and would tell me how glad she was to see me. Sadly, Janine moved away that summer and it would be years before I ever stepped foot inside that big white chapel again. When I was ten years old, missionaries taught me the discussions and soon thereafter I was baptized. And it all began with Janine—a little girl who never knew that what she did changed my life forever.

Few phrases perk up the ears of Church members more quickly than "Let me tell you a story." Illustrations in the form of a narrative have been told for thousands of years—at the seashore, around the campfire, at the dinner table. Some stories fit in better than others with the traditions and expectations of sacrament meeting.

Some stories deserve to be told and retold as they define how we see ourselves as Latter-day Saints. These include stories such as the First Vision, the publishing of the Book of Mormon and the pioneer trek. Other stories are unique in nature and are used to make a specific point. Both can work in a sacrament meeting talk if carefully crafted and told with warmth.

If you're going to use a story to illustrate a point, be selective in the account you choose. Sources for true stories include yourself, family, neighbors, newspapers, Church history, biographies and scriptures. Keep in mind, just because it happened to you, doesn't mean you can tell the story well or that it will naturally make a clear point. The key is in the telling.

Make sure you can answer these questions:

Why are you telling this story?
What is the point?
What are the who, what, when, where and why elements?
What were the sights, sounds, tastes and smells?
What was the problem?
How was it solved?
What did you (or someone else) learn? ("And thus we see . . . ")

Stories, when used in a sermon, need to be pruned to the barest essential elements. Create "nutrient dense stories"—narratives with the most important information compacted into the fewest words. Practice the story out loud with a stopwatch or clock to determine how long it takes to tell. Stories that drag on often cause talks to go overtime and then there is insufficient time to draw the spiritual conclusion that is needed. The summation is usually the most significant component and if it is shriveled due to timing, the story will be robbed of its impact. Plan ahead to include stories that will support your overall objective.

Can Humor Fit In?

A merry heart doeth good like a medicine.

Proverbs 17:22

Considering the sacred nature of sacrament meeting, it is inappropriate to drop in the latest one-liner picked up from late-night television. Nor does a new joke from the Internet really match the tone of sacrament meeting. We do not gather to be entertained, we gather to be strengthened, enlightened and inspired. So, is laughter ever welcome?

To be honest, life is funny. There were probably days when Nephi was building the ship that both he and his brothers fell on the ground cracking up. Whenever you try to build something the first time, some part usually gets attached backward, upside down or inside out. The ability to look at your own blunders and missteps and find humor rather than humiliation is a positive attribute and a real stress reliever. Telling those kind of stories, when they support the point you're trying to make, can elicit sympathetic laughter and a wonderful sense of bonding.

This is *emergent humor*—something that happens naturally in the telling of an engaging personal story. Maybe it happens in the middle of the story, maybe at the end. The story was included for a clear purpose beyond its humorous aspect. If laughter arises, fine. If ward members miss the humor, that's OK too. There's no big punch line awkwardly punctuated by a long empty pause.

Sometimes in the telling of stories, laughter erupts unexpectedly. Smile, pause and enjoy the warm response of those listening to you. Never let an appropriate giggle rippling through the congregation break your concentration. Stay on message. The Lord may have been pleasantly surprised at Abraham's response to the news that he was to become a Father. "Then Abraham fell upon his face, and laughed, and said in his heart, Shall a child be born unto him that is an hundred years old?" (GENESIS 17:17) In spite of Abraham's reaction, it appears the message was delivered in its entirety and a covenant fulfilled—a good example.

Stories Touch Hearts

O Lord, I have heard thy speech, and was afraid.

Habakkuk 3:2

"They brought Daniel, and cast him into the den of lions. Now the king spake and said unto Daniel, Thy God whom thou servest continually, he will deliver thee" (Daniel 6:16). Even though you know how it ends, when the story of faithful Daniel and his unfair imprisonment is told well, you can't help being caught up in the reality of what he faced. How would it have felt? His emotions become yours.

Stories with a strong emotional framework can convey strong emotional appeal in a memorable way. You may be tempted to shy away from stories like that—but used appropriately they can be powerful. Fear. Anger. Hatred. Love. Mercy. A well-told super-charged emotional narrative can take the listener to a place they have never gone personally, but can visit through your story. The emotions play out through characters that are actual, personal, scriptural, allegorical, fictional and historical. Used carefully, they can add depth and warmth to a sacrament meeting talk. But there are certain criteria that influence whether or not it would be appropriate in sacrament meeting.

Actual. If it's a contemporary story, and it's not about you and your family, do you have personal knowledge of its veracity? The Internet is flooded with stories that are pure baloney. People tend to resist emotional stories that are fabricated, particularly if they are presented as fact. If you can't establish the facts, avoid the story altogether.

Personal. Your personal stories are easiest to tell. But make sure you do not let the emotions of the story get the best of you. This is not the time to feel the emotion yourself; it is the time to convey it to others. Rehearsal will allow you to keep your feelings under control.

Scriptural. There are plenty of stories from the scriptures, that when fleshed out a bit, are exquisitely emotive. The raising of the daughter of Jairus. The widow's mite. The prodigal son. The good Samaritan. The assistance of Rahab. Peter's denial of Christ. Drawing parallels with today is not difficult when the story is told from a contemporaneous perspective. Tell it as if you were there.

Allegorical. There are numerous stories told through the ages about animals, trees, clouds, ants, etc. These can be woven in for the purpose of making a point. No one ever mistakes them for being true and the point is always clear. Choose carefully. Avoid stories that involve mystical or magical elements as they rarely involve the Spirit.

Fictional. This is an area that can be more complicated, but can be effectively used if done so thoughtfully. Whether from a movie or a novel, characters can reveal gospel principles in a poignant way. However, it may be wise to avoid characters from movies and novels not widely known or inappropriate for a great majority of the congregation.

Historical. Whether from Church history or world history, it is easy to be caught up in the drama and emotion of inspiring events. Founding fathers, war heroes, ancestors, inventors, authors, prophets, missionaries—all have great stories with positive spiritual lessons.

Stories unite us by allowing us to cry together. They are an emotional superglue that makes us one.

Use Names Reverently

In the name of Jesus Christ of Nazareth rise up and walk.

Acts 3:6

Names have power and significance. We show reverence by how we refer to people, organizations and leaders. Sometimes we are under the mistaken notion that giving nicknames shows that we are insiders and have an especially close relationship. When it comes to the domain of the sacred, nicknames are out of place.

All you have to do is remember that one child in your neighborhood that was always picked on. Was it the nickname that caused the behavior? Or the behavior that generated the nickname? It probably doesn't matter which came first. Both were negative and un-Christlike. I remember always feeling strange and uncomfortable about calling my neighbor's little sister "Moochie," even though I was never told any other name to call her. She was small and frail and extremely withdrawn. She moved away before I ever learned her real name. I hope she escaped the nickname's impact at her next neighborhood.

Using names as they are given is respectful, fully appropriate and expected from the pulpit. One of the greatest examples of reverence toward a name comes from The First Vision. "One of them spake unto me, calling me by name" (JS—H 1:17).

Nicknames. Become aware of how you describe sacred things—both at home and at the pulpit. Make sure you show reverence by the words you choose. Certain abbreviations and nicknames have crept into the vocabulary of some and do not belong in private conversation or in a sacrament meeting talk. Examine the way you speak and be sure that the words you use show reverence. Eliminate any words that show disrespect or casualness toward the sacred. *Examples*: B of M, D&C, Bish, GAs, Prez, the Scrips, Sticks, Mish, Greenie, Comp.

Mispronounced words. Another way of showing respect for both sacred text and your listeners is to be mindful of words that are often mispronounced. To avoid mispronouncing some of the more unfamiliar Book of Mormon names, refer to the Pronouncing Guide found at the end of the Book of Mormon. Here is a sampling of commonly mispronounced words with the most-accented pronunciation:

Arimathea (AIR uh muth EE uh)
Bethlehem (BETH luh hem)
Chemish (KEM ish)
Genealogy (jehn ee ALL o gee)
Habakkuk (huh BAK kuhk)
Immanuel (im MAN yoo el)
Melchizedek (mel KIZ eh dek)
Nebuchadnezzar (neb uh kuhd NEZ uhr)
Paradisiacal (pair uh dih SIE ih kul)
Patriarchal (pay tree ARE kul)
Philemon (fie LEE muhn)
Sinai (SIE nie)
Tamar (TAY mar)
Zeezrom (zee EZ rum)

In addition to showing reverence, you will also discover that by learning the most accepted pronunciation before you speak, you will be less likely to stumble over a difficult word. As you practice the pronunciation you will be able to speak with greater authority and confidence.

Avoiding nicknames and striving to pronounce names properly adds depth and credibility. The realm of the sacred demands formality and care; by showing appropriate concern for names you communicate reverence for the message you are sharing.

Organize
Your Ideas

You, who are the first laborers in this last kingdom assemble yourselves together, and organize yourselves.

Doctrine and Covenants 88:74

We Need Order

For all things must be done in order.

Doctrine and Covenants 28:13

In some foreign countries, traffic signs and traffic laws are routinely ignored. It's as if there are no lines painted on the road and no concern for anyone else's safety or well being. Taxi rides feel like "Mr. Toad's Wild Ride" without the benefit of knowing that in 90 seconds you'll be escorted back into Disneyland. Many drivers appear to be competing in a demolition derby you hope to survive. There is total disregard for the simplest of common courtesies. Chaos prevails.

It seems a strange circumstance for the 21st century, but it exists nonetheless. This makes getting from point A to point B dangerous, frustrating and exhausting. No one wants to live in a world like that for very long. There is a deep yearning in the human heart for order.

That yearning applies to messages delivered at Church also. Sacrament meeting sermons benefit from being carefully organized. Organize your thoughts in a way that is easy for ward members to understand. As the congregation nods and smiles, staying with you throughout the duration of your talk, you feel a surge of confidence and a sense of accomplishment.

Remember—sometimes what is referred to as boring, is simply disorganized. A few minutes of scrutiny and reassembling can turn verbal pandemonium into verbal paradise. But it has to be done in advance.

The following is a typical outline of a sacrament meeting talk. It allows infinite variations, but is easy to create, modify and use. It is also a format that is easily followed by listeners. It is designed for three main points, but adapts easily for 2–5 points.

Introduction
    Transition to Body
        1st Main Point with Supporting Sub-Points (as needed)
        2nd Main Point with Supporting Sub-Points (as needed)
        3rd Main Point with Supporting Sub-Points (as needed)
    Transition to Conclusion
Conclusion and Testimony

What follows is a brief description of each portion so you can see their purpose and what they should include.

Introduction: This draws listeners into your topic. It will be about 10 percent of your talk.

Transition to Body: Alerts the audience that the main information is commencing.

1st Main Point: Normally you will have 2–5 main points. Select the order that will make sense to your listeners. Organize thoughtfully rather than randomly.

Supporting Sub-Points: Select support material from a vast array of possibilities: Words of the prophets, scriptures, examples, stories, personal experiences, quotes, hypothetical situations, poetry, journal entries, hymns, scientific findings, current events, or interviews. Don't overdo it. Choose the best.

2nd Main Point with Supporting Sub-Points (Repeat pattern above)
3rd Main Point with Supporting Sub-Points (Repeat pattern above)

Transition to Conclusion: This alerts listeners that the conclusion is coming.

Conclusions and Testimony: It will be about 10 percent of your talk and will include a recap of main points, the message you want listeners to remember and your personal testimony.

What Are the Questions?

When your children ask their fathers in time to come, saying, What mean ye by these stones? Then ye shall answer them.

Joshua 4:6–7

One of the great things about having young children around the house is being peppered with questions all day long. They are determined to understand how the world functions and you become the source of all truth. "Where do the butterflies go?" "How come the moon looks like that?" "Does Heavenly Father know who I am?"

A carefully prepared speaker tries to predict the questions that will occur in the minds of listeners. In many topics, particularly stories from the scriptures, there are questions that naturally emerge. If you think in the order that listeners will be thinking, you can logically arrange your ideas based on their questions.

Layer One: The first and most easily answered questions reflect the details of the story: *Who? What? When? Where?* As simple as they may be, answering these questions may still require significant study. The more background you can find, the more the story comes to life and it becomes clear that these were real events that happened to real people. There are numerous sources that can help add this kind of depth. However, information like this is simply for the purpose of piquing interest in deeper exploration. Make your sentences verbally dense, including as many essential details as possible. Drop the superfluous or unnecessary, as it will bog down the story.

Layer Two: Beneath the first layer comes the second layer of questions: *How? Why?* Sometimes these can be answered, sometimes not. The search, however, is still valuable and creates a sense of connection. The best source for the ideas discussed here will be the scriptures and the words of the prophets.

The Core: Next, you make it to the central and most powerful question: *What does it mean?* Here's where you can explore your experience with the gospel principle or scripture story. Embedded in the meaning is the added layer of application. You are never really finished exploring a gospel topic until you examine and discuss how to apply it. Your experience and testimony add weight to the discussion.

Organizing your ideas based on questions makes it easy to construct your talk. It also makes it easier for members of the ward to follow your ideas. Let them know if there is a question you've deliberately left unanswered. This may cause them to explore the topic further.

In the Beginning

In the beginning was the Word,
and the Word was with God,
and the Word was God.

John 1:1

It's frustrating but true. Within the first few minutes of a job interview a potential employer determines whether your application will go into the paper shredder or if you will be considered for hiring. This decision is often made before your impressive experience or vital skills are even discussed. Some research indicates that a negative decision can be made in as little as seven seconds. Ouch.

Ward members are typically more generous than interviewers. But a well-constructed and warmly delivered introduction is still essential as listeners decide during those first few moments how valuable they think your message will be and adjust their attentiveness accordingly. You can put them on the edge of their seats, or you can put them to sleep.

Your job is to make them hungry for the delicious message you have prepared. There are five tasks a well-written introduction performs. Through your opening words you will *connect, attract, reveal, establish* and *map.*

Connect. Build a relationship with your audience with your initial greeting and smile. Find a common ground.

Attract. Gain listeners' attention and draw them into your topic, by explaining the topic's value, importance and urgency.

Reveal. Introduce your topic thoughtfully. You may want to mention your central message.

Establish. Introduce a reason to take your message seriously, whether it's your research, experience or testimony.

Map. Preview the main points and transition to the body of your talk.

A typical introduction will only represent about ten percent of your talk, perhaps a minute or two in total. But it is such a significant portion, and can make such difference, that it should be given substantial attention.

When creating your sermon, it is advisable to delay writing your introduction until you are totally certain of your mission, message and main points. Then you can be assured that your introduction will support your objective. For a sense of continuity, write your conclusion at the same time.

Well-written and carefully rehearsed, an introduction has the potential of gaining the undivided attention of ward members. You can then alert them to be aware of inspiration that could remain with them for the rest of their lives.

Connect through a Salutation

When Elisabeth heard the salutation of Mary,
the babe leaped in her womb;
and Elisabeth was filled with the Holy Ghost.

Luke 1:41

Western civilization has become, in many ways, increasingly *un*civilized. Daily immersed in this fast-paced and progressively more impersonal environment, you can easily embrace the get-the-job-done-hang-the-simple-courtesies mentality that has overrun much of our interpersonal communication. Just think of emails received in the last week—how many of them had a personal salutation?

When you stand at the pulpit, extend a greeting to the congregation. You are telling the members of the ward that they are the specific recipients of a message prepared especially for them. This can be a profoundly important step. The first words you speak set the tone and determine to a certain degree how your message will be received. Everyone wants to feel included.

Consider the greetings typically used in your ward. If one feels comfortable, use it. If not, create your own. The key is to make it warm, sincere and comfortable. This is your first opportunity to really connect and let the members of the ward know that you created your message with them in mind.

For a salutation, you have plenty of options from which to choose as the list below indicates:

"My dear brethren and sisters . . . "
"Good afternoon, brothers and sisters . . . "
"It's good to be with you this morning . . . "
"Greetings my fellow brothers and sisters . . . "
"My beloved brothers and sisters . . . "
"What a wonderful meeting this has been so far, brother and sisters . . . "
"Brothers and sisters, I come to you this afternoon with . . . "

Your purpose is to create an environment that is conducive to receiving your sermon. Do it with an affectionate and spiritual tone.

As you look out into the faces of the congregation and greet them with a warm salutation, you will feel connected to them and they will feel connected to you. What a great way to begin a message! "That your incomings may be in the name of the Lord; that your outgoings may be in the name of the Lord; that all your salutations may be in the name of the Lord" (D&C 88:120).

Keep the Connection

Say unto your brethren in Zion,
in love greeting, that I have called you.

Doctrine and Covenants 90:32

After you greet the congregation, launch full steam ahead into your introduction. Include all the components you feel are necessary. Make your introduction energetic and warm. This is when you crank up the magnetic power that will pull listeners into your message.

Love. Begin with a spirit of love for the members of the ward. Your tender feelings will come across in a way that radiates warmth and light—in fact, you'll become a *human light bulb*. Christlike love is the result of special spiritual preparation, as outlined by the prophet Moroni. It takes supreme effort, but will influence your delivery in a wonderful way. "Pray unto the Father with all the energy of heart, that ye may be filled with this love" (Moroni 7:48).

Smile. This is the universal facial expression that communicates "I like you." It immediately prepares people to hear a positive message. Speaking anxiety can erase the smile that normally is found on your face. You may want to practice in the mirror to remember what a smile feels like so you can nudge it to the surface if you feel a bit anxious. A smile will actually help put you at ease also—so it does double duty.

Include. A feeling of mutual support can emerge when expressions of the common human condition make it clear that everyone is still progressing and no one has arrived. Use inclusive language like *we, us* and *our* whenever you can. Be especially aware of reducing the number of times you use *I, me* and *my*. The "we're-all-in-this-together" mentality communicates a feeling of humility and a desire for mutual growth.

Know. You need to know where you're headed and convey that feeling in the energy you communicate. Ward members will sense the electricity and be eager to *plug in* to your ideas.

You will forge a human link with everyone in your line of sight as you inform them that your message is designed to bless them. Make it clear that you care about their spiritual and temporal well being.

One warning: Everything positive you have accomplished up to this point will be sabotaged if you launch into a litany of apologies or excuses. By doing so, you communicate weakness, a lack of preparation and minimal concern for the audience—the complete opposite of your intention. Before you begin speaking, compensate for whatever road blocks or problems that have arisen so you can stand with confidence and deliver the message you prepared.

Attract Your Audience

He layeth down his own life that he may draw all men unto him.

2 Nephi 26:24

While sitting in the sand of the elementary school playground, I loved to drag a magnet endlessly through the grains of sand. The magnet would emerge completely coated in iron filings, looking like a strange, black, furry alien. No matter how many times I went through the pile of sand there was always more to be found. I was astounded at the endless power of the magnet to pull the iron from the sand.

Can you magnetize your message? It is essential to draw listeners into your topic. Do not assume that because they are at Church that they will naturally be interested in what you have to say. Instead, put yourself in the place of ward members and ask yourself what would help make the topic come alive. This is an important strategy, but use only one, or at most two, of the following ideas to magnetize your message.

Startle. An astonishing quote, a chilling passage from a journal, the details from an amazing current event, or a frightening statistic, used appropriately, can jolt listeners from their complacent seats into a realization that the topic is important. President Gordon B. Hinckley has used this technique as a means of calling our attention to problems of our day: "In 1994 alone, Americans spent 482 billion dollars on gambling—more than they spent that year on movies, sports, music, cruise ships, and theme parks combined."[1]

Question. You can easily engage listeners by presenting a question for their consideration. This forces them to come up with a suitable answer in their minds, in much the same way they would answer in a personal conversation. By redirecting their thinking, you can utilize their natural inquisitiveness to lead them to the answers. There are a number of effective types of questions that can be used. Develop a question that will urge listeners to pay attention to answers that you have found.

"What would happen if . . . ?"
"How do you respond when someone . . . ?"
"What did the Savior do when He was faced with . . . ?"
"What does the Lord suggest . . . ?"
"How can you find the answer to . . . ?"

Personalize. Everyone wants to know that the issue being discussed affects them personally. And the closer you can get in time and space, the better. Basically, your target is "here and now." Use an example that places the situation at everyone's front door today. If you've had a recent experience that applies, this could be a good time to mention it.

Claim. State the importance, magnitude and urgency of the issue. Back up your claim with information from a credible and respected source. Be aware of how the source is viewed by ward members. On spiritual matters, the Lord's prophet has far more credibility than a national talk show host or political figure.

Warn. Using this strategy you outline the negative consequences or risks associated with not making the right choice or the blessings and benefits that come with choosing the right path. Paint the images with crystal clear imagery. The Savior did this effectively in his final chastisement of the Pharisees in the 23rd chapter of Matthew. "Ye generation of vipers, how can ye escape the damnation of hell? (MATTHEW 23:33)

Intrigue. Tell a story that draws the audience into the issue and makes them care about the outcome. You may find it effective to only tell them half the story, leaving them wondering about the ending until the conclusion of your talk. *Note:* If you use this strategy, don't forget to wrap things up at the end.

These strategies allow for infinite variety and guarantee you'll never need to use the same story or quote twice. Allow this list to help you generate lots of ideas for getting the audience engaged.

Note

1. *Standing for Something* (2000), xxi.

Reveal Your Topic

Reveal unto them the abundance of peace and truth.

Jeremiah 33:6

Once in a restaurant in France, a meal was presented to me that was mysteriously nestled underneath a delicate silver dome. The elegance of the location combined with the tantalizing aromas, elevated the anticipation. On cue, the wait staff simultaneously lifted the domes with a whispered chorus of "*Voilà!*" Our gasps were audible and our applause spontaneous and sincere. I remember few details of the meal, but I do remember the drama of that moment. My desire to enjoy every delectable morsel was multiplied by the careful and dramatic presentation.

While this model may be a bit extravagant when considering how to reveal the topic you plan to discuss in your talk, it is difficult to explain how the opposite has become the norm. Somehow, the default disclosure has become, "The topic I have been assigned is . . . " While this may accomplish the task of announcing the subject matter, the focus remains on you rather than on the audience. That will not generate high voltage attention—it won't even generate static electricity.

Remember, a sermon is for the congregation—not for you. Your comments should be designed to get the audience as enthusiastic about your message as you are. Once you've drawn the audience in, you want to reveal the topic in a way that makes them feel this is a custom-designed sermon just for them. Find a way to focus the attention back on the audience. *Voilà!*

Find a lead-in sentence that does the job. It may take some work, but you'll be glad you took the extra effort. Here are some idea-starters.

"You may find it helpful to learn more about . . . "
"If you're like me, you've often wondered . . . "
"I was surprised when I discovered . . . "
"The prophet Nephi wrestled with the same problem . . . "
"Even while on the cross, the Savior . . . "

If you can reveal the topic in such a way as to maintain the energy you've already created, then you have succeeded.

Establish Credibility

Go forth among thy brethren, and establish my word.

Alma 17:11

Credibility is the audience's perception of whether or not you are fully truthful. Maybe that seems an odd issue to discuss within the context of speaking in Church—but maybe it's more important here than anywhere else. Eternal salvation hangs in the balance.

The key is to subtly include those bits of information that will enhance your credibility and by extension enhance the authority of your message. Listeners will gently process your message and your credibility simultaneously and make a decision as you finish as to whether or not to accept your message.

You contribute to listeners' perception of your credibility through your enthusiasm, research, background and testimony.

Your enthusiasm. You show through your word choice, delivery and energy that you believe what you are saying is both true and important. Never show a tepid or halfhearted position—people want conviction.

Your information and research. Listeners expect, and rightfully so, that you have gone to great lengths to extract the most valuable and reliable information available on this topic. You may not be the world's most renowned expert, but you have gone to those who are. Use the names of those whose words and ideas support the points you are making.

Your background and experience. If a past Church calling, assignment, leadership position, mission, career, volunteer experience, summer job, hobby or talent relates directly to the topic at hand, you can gently weave it into the fabric of your talk to build the listeners' respect for your opinion.

Your testimony. Make sure the ward knows how you feel about the topic, what your personal testimony is and how you gained it. Your personal journey to this particular spiritual knowledge may be life-changing for some who hear you testify.

The presence of the Holy Spirit. Ultimately, the presence of the Holy Spirit is the single most important factor. If what you say is true, your message will be confirmed by the Holy Ghost. He is a testator of truth. He provides the highest level of credibility.

Give Listeners a Road Map

And it came to pass that there arose a mist of darkness . . . insomuch that they who had commenced in the path did lose their way.

1 Nephi 8:23

How hard could it be to get home? Just jump on Interstate 5 and drive north. Olympia to Seattle. No need for a map. It had been an exhausting day at the capitol, trying to affect pending legislation and build alliances. A typically dark and dreary Northwest sky was draped overhead. It was time to get in the old red Volvo station wagon and return home. All I had to do was get up the on-ramp and start the long journey. Hard to believe that an intelligent person could go 30 miles in the wrong direction, but I did. I didn't have a map and I wasn't familiar with any landmarks that would have indicated that I was heading in the opposite direction. I was almost to Oregon before I turned around.

Most listeners, if they get lost during your sermon, will simply tune you out. It's not mean-spirited; it's a fact of life. Trying to find your way in a confusing sermon without a mental map is tiring and fatigue can overtake even the most devoted listener.

Right before you launch into the main body of your sermon, give ward members an idea of where you will be going. What are some of the places you'll be visiting along the way? How many stops will you be making? What are some interesting things to watch for? What is the final destination? This builds interest and allows listeners to envision the whole trip.

These comments should be the last part of your introduction so it can provide a smooth lead-in to the body. *Warning:* Don't make your "road map" so detailed that the audience feels they've already made the trip. Your comments should be more like a travel brochure which gets your listeners excited about the trip. Once they get on board, your job is to remain faithful to the road map you provided.

Make It Hard to Get Lost

He said unto them:
Behold, I give unto you a sign.

Helaman 14:2

As a child, long road trips quickly became tedious with repetitive desert scenery and no air conditioning. One thing which helped me sense some degree of progress was the ubiquitous sequence of Burma Shave signs on the side of the road. I didn't always understand them—but I always read them. They made me feel I was getting closer to my destination.

She kissed the hairbrush
By mistake
She thought it was
Her husband Jake
Burma Shave

One of the most confusing aspects of listening to someone else's talk is to figure out how far into their sermon they are—information which gives a clue as to how close to finishing they might be. Most listeners appreciate being given signposts along the way. In your introduction you give a map of where you're headed, then as you pass certain mile posts you need to point out your progress. Mileage markers or landmarks in your sermon allow the audience to feel movement toward the conclusion. When people get lost during a sermon, they lose interest and drift off.

Mileage Markers

Provide a system that works for you and for those who will be listening. Let your listeners know how many main points you'll be discussing. Verbal mileage markers or sign posts alert the audience as you discuss each one. This provides a sense of progress toward a final destination.

Numbers. This is the simplest to do and the easiest for the audience to follow. Everyone likes to know how many miles ahead. "These six things doth the Lord hate: yea, seven are an abomination unto him" (PROVERBS 6:1). If you have three points, begin section one with *first,* section two with *second,* and section three with *finally*. Using the word *finally* instead of *third* lets the audience know that you've reached your last main point and that you're not going to add an extra one at the last minute.

Questions. You can use questions at the beginning of each main point. It makes the audience think about the topic as you prepare to launch into the discussion. If you were going to discuss the Prophet Joseph in Liberty Jail, you might want to mention his arrest, the Saints' persecution, the suffering of the Prophet, and the sacred words that resulted. These four questions could launch each main point.

1. Why was the Prophet arrested?
2. What happened to the Saints while Joseph languished in jail?
3. What happened to Joseph in Liberty Jail?
4. What sacred words resulted from that dark and dirty dungeon?

Key words. "The Primary colors are one, two, three, red, yellow and blue . . . " You can start off a section with a key word. "Red is for courage." This is a good strategy when the audience knows or can easily remember the key words. Parts of familiar scripture passages or hymns work well also.

Be sure to honor the original "road map," avoiding side trips and detours that could be confusing. The message the audience wants to hear is, "Welcome, you have arrived." You don't actually say it in so many words, but you let them know that you hit every main point that was described in the beginning. Recap what they now understand, so they can celebrate the accomplishment with you.

Rule of Three

And now abideth faith, hope, charity, these three.

1 Corinthians 13:13

CHOCOLATE, VANILLA AND STRAWBERRY. Red, white and blue. Gold, silver and bronze. Much of the world seems to be organized in groups of three—an organization that is ideally suited to the brain's storage system. Retrieval of words, ideas, even numbers are easiest in groups of three. When you're driving down the highway, notice how many states have chosen a combination of three numbers and three letters on their license plates. There's a reason. Police officers can remember and recite the groups of three more easily and with fewer errors.

When creating main points or sub-points for your talk, choosing three can be helpful for both you and the audience. Make certain that the points are fairly equal in importance and content. Avoid having two strong points and one flimsy add-on. Use the Rule of Three when it makes sense, but don't artificially impose it on your talk.

Another use is when you list attributes, attitudes or actions in your talk.

"She was shy, awkward and tongue-tied."
"Go forth with power, purpose and peace."
"When building a fire you need to gather tinder, kindling and fuel."

The ear has been trained since childhood to listen for information in groups of three: Stop, look and listen! Take full advantage of the Rule of Three when developing your message.

Some of the most easily recognized groupings in the scriptures are groups of three. Consider these:

Father, Son and Holy Ghost
Shadrach, Meshach and Abednego
Shem, Ham and Japheth
Laman, Lemuel and Nephi
Gold, frankincense and myrrh
Celestial, telestial and terrestrial
Peter, James and John
Glory of the sun, moon and stars
Deacon, teacher and priest
Preach the gospel, perfect the Saints and redeem the dead
Faith, hope and charity

If you have doubts about the veracity of the Rule of Three, just try naming all four sons of Mosiah! Your goal is to have your message remembered by your listeners, so you may want to find ways to use the Rule of Three.

Choose the Best Order

The steps of a good man are ordered by the Lord: and he delighteth in his way.
Psalm 37:23

Saturdays are often filled with a long list of errands to run—grocery shopping, soccer game, service project, library, repair shop, computer store, piano lesson, dry cleaner. When thought about logically and in advance, time, frustration and gasoline can be saved by doing the trips in a specific sequence. Done randomly, the list might never be completed. If you organize your list in the best order, the task is a breeze. Planning is the key.

There is a best order for the main points of your talk also. Don't just settle for the order in which they occurred to you. To do so will create an organization that is haphazard and lacking in meaning. Ask yourself if there is a way to organize them that will make it easier to follow and easier to remember. As you keep your audience in mind, you will find the best way to arrange your main points. Consider your topic, mission, message and audience as you study the four organization strategies that follow. Ask yourself if the message you are developing would respond well to one of these.

Chronological. Organize your main points in time sequence. The organization will reflect the order of an historical event or the steps in a process. This is one of the easiest and most natural ways to organize a talk. *Example:* The First Vision.

Cause and effect. Organize your main points into two parts with the first section discussing behavior patterns, positive or negative, and the second section containing the results. *Example:* Viewing of pornography and its destructive impact.

Problem and solution. Organize your main points into two parts, the first section discussing a problem or issue and the second section describing what can be done to correct, mitigate or solve. *Example:* Disharmony in the home and strategies to create an environment of peace.

Scriptural framework. Organize your main points using the keywords of a scripture passage. *Example:* The Woman of Samaria comes to a progressively deeper testimony of the Savior, referring to Him as 1) Jew; 2) Sir; 3) prophet; 4) the Christ (JOHN 4). *Example:* Paul summarizes the steps of a valiant life as 1) Fought the good fight; 2) Finished my course; 3) Kept the faith; 4) Crown of righteousness (2 TIMOTHY 4:7–8).

The Lord will help you find the best way to organize your ideas. Once you have settled on an organization that feels right, you will find it is easier to remember the order and give your talk a sense of flow. "Order my steps in thy word" (PSALM 119:133).

From Milk to Meat

I have fed you with milk, and not with meat: for hitherto ye were not able to bear it.

1 Corinthians 3:2

Just as babies start with milk and eventually move to meat, those listening to you will appreciate it if you start with the simplest concepts—those that everyone can easily understand—and then move carefully and deliberately toward the more complex or difficult. Of course, that doesn't mean you have to move to the incomprehensible.

When the ideas flow in an escalating manner, building upon the previous one, you increase the likelihood that people will stay with you and not get confused. Here are some examples to get you on the right wavelength. The order of your main points can really make a difference.

As you consider your mission and your message, your main points will begin to form in your mind. Write them in pencil, because initially the list will be rather fluid and changeable. As you study the topic, your main points will shift, change and evolve. Organize them in the order that will be easiest to follow. Sometimes organization will be intuitive and main points will seem to self-organize. Points can be organized a number of ways. Choose one that works for your talk.

Simple to complex. Move step by step from a basic to a more complex view. *Example:* Discuss the principle of doing work by proxy, starting with a stunt double in a movie, then a proxy ballot, then temple work, then the Atonement.

Easy to difficult. Move step by step from the easy to do to the more challenging. *Example:* To speak about what it takes to build an eternal family can start with mentioning attending Church together, then teaching one another, then forgiving one anther, then working on a long-term service project together, and serving one who is preparing to die.

Familiar to unfamiliar. Move step-by-step from the comfortable to the awkward or uneasy. *Example:* Talk about learning how to do missionary work by discussing Family Home Evening, then teaching a Sunday School class, and finally proselytizing in a foreign country.

Small to large. Move step by step from the minor and easily embraced to the major and more difficult to embrace. *Example:* To teach the law of consecration, you could start with tithing a child's 50-cent allowance, move to giving a generous fast offering, and conclude with serving a full-time senior mission.

Ancient to modern. Move step by step through examples from the ancient world to modern applications. *Example:* With the topic of fasting you could easily discuss the story of Esther, then the example of the Savior, and then an example from Church history.

General to specific. Move step by step from a universal principle toward a more focused application. *Example:* If you were discussing obedience, you might discuss the general obedience of City of Enoch and the specific obedience of Joseph of Egypt. You can also move from the specific of personal righteousness being the first step to a community of Saints.

The progressions seems natural enough in these cases, but you can miss an opportunity to make your message easier to latch onto if you don't look carefully at the potential for organizing your main points in this way. It doesn't always work, but when it does, it is helpful for both speaker and listener.

Don't Wander Off Course

I have finished my course, I have kept the faith.

2 Timothy 4:7

After a late afternoon solo climb up a heavily forested mountain trail in the Cascades, I sat on the peak to drink in the beauty of the valley below. The sun was sinking low on the horizon, and I knew it would be important to start down right away. Without thinking, I jumped up and started down the path in front of me. Unfortunately, it was not the path that led back down the mountain. Gravity pulled me downhill quickly until I reached the terminus of the trail. It was a camp site at the edge of a steep drop-off, not the parking lot.

By not staying on the path that would lead to my destination, I had veered off in an unplanned direction. I had to retrace my steps, climbing for a second time to the summit, in order to get back to my car. As the sky darkened, I began to realize the kind of jeopardy I had exposed myself to by wandering off course. I was running out of time. It was going to be even harder to reach my destination.

Listeners love to know what the ultimate destination is and then hear the speaker take the most direct path to that destination. It's almost an unspoken contract between speaker and listener. When a speaker is "winging it," or in other words, drifting from one loosely connected subject to another, it makes it difficult for the audience to pin down what the actual subject matter is or if there is a desired outcome. They can't see the desired destination. And that could be because the speaker never chose one. Or if one was chosen, it was abandoned along the way.

Choose a destination, then stay the course.

Steps to Conclude

Ye are blessed, for the testimony which ye have borne is recorded in heaven for the angels to look upon.

Doctrine and Covenants 62:3

"The land of the free and the home of the brave." That's the one line of the "Star-spangled Banner" that everyone knows. For most, that's the line that defines the message of the national anthem.

The final words you speak will determine, to a large extent, what message your listeners will remember. Your conclusion will package a number of interrelated steps that will make it possible for your audience to take home the message you have designed for them.

A well-written conclusion must perform five tasks. As you write the conclusion of your message, you will *signal, reinforce, restate, close* and *seal.* Examine the purpose of each task to identify what words you are choosing to accomplish them. Each task deserves specific attention, although that may not mean creating a lot of text. Eventually the steps will come to you instinctively.

Signal: Alert your listeners that the end of your talk is approaching by using words, body language and voice. Listeners love to hear "In conclusion . . ." or something similar. This is where you transition from the body of your talk to the conclusion.

Reinforce: Reconnect with ideas in your introduction. You may want to complete the second half of a story you began in the introduction or mention an additional fact, scripture or quote that underscores the value, importance or urgency of your message.

Restate: Reinforce your message; never leave listeners wondering what your point is.

Close: Encourage your listeners to ponder, remember, feel or act.

Seal: Bear your testimony of the principle you've discussed, then close in the name of the Savior. Your impact will be increased if your final words are spoken slowly and deliberately, while looking at ward members rather than your notes.

One important hint. Avoid adding new material during the conclusion. Even if you forgot to mention something important, under most circumstances once you have initiated the conclusion sequence you need to stick with the concepts you have already covered. If you do squeeze something in, it creates a sense of confusion and disorder. Chances are the new material won't be remembered and it may diminish the chance that your message will be remembered.

Signal the End Is Near

For behold, the time draweth near,
and the end soon cometh.

Jacob 5:29

The problem for Chicken Little was that the sky wasn't falling. If he'd been right, that would have been important information.

Likewise, your listeners always love to know the end is coming. Not because they didn't enjoy your message—but because they did. And they want to remember it. Listening to a sermon requires the audience to manage their attentiveness. Listening is a selective behavior and some may fade in and out due to various distractions. By signaling that the conclusion is coming, they will be at maximum alertness so they can be prepared with an appropriate reaction or response.

So what do you do to let them know you're ready to wrap up? Word choice, voice speed and pitch, eye contact, handling of visual aids and body positioning.

Word choice. Audiences crave hearing those blessed words, "In conclusion," or any number of similar phrases. It's the clearest trigger that the speaker is going to review the main points and tell listeners what course of action to take.

Voice speed. Slow down a bit, without dragging. While enthusiasm is a valuable asset in any sermon, this is where you calm down just a bit and reinforce your sincerity and credibility.

Voice pitch. Move lower, just a notch. This also enhances your perceived sincerity and credibility. It is not an affectation, but a natural tone of voice that exudes confidence and calm.

Eye contact. As you launch into the conclusion you should look up almost all the time. This is your final opportunity to bond with your listeners and urge them to embrace the principle you spoke about. This clearly demands that you have the content well-rehearsed. This will give your final words the added solemnity and authenticity that comes from speaking rather than reading.

Handling of visual aids. If you have scriptures or another object in your hand, this is the time to set it down. The conclusion is a time to recap ideas in a general way, so you should not need to refer to lengthy passages of scriptures.

Body positioning. Finally, straighten up and speak to the center of the chapel. Up to this point, you may have been speaking to one section or another, but this is the time to be facing forward and letting everyone know you're ready to conclude.

Reinforce Your Message

Behold, I make an end of speaking concerning this people.

Mormon 8:13

This is the moment where you commend your listeners for paying attention until the end by reminding them of the value of the message and how it will benefit their lives. You will reinforce, restate and close your message.

Reinforce

You can do this easily by reconnecting with ideas in your introduction. You will clarify for your listeners the importance, urgency and value of your message.

Second half of story. If you leave a story incomplete in the introduction, this is where you reveal the resolution, showing the value of the principle in bringing about a pleasant conclusion.

Additional fact or statistic. This reminds listeners of the importance or urgency of the issue.

Quote from a credible voice. Your claim of an issue's significance is enhanced by using the authority of a highly respected person.

Restate

In conjunction reinforcing the value of the ideas you presented, you will restate the message you want the audience to remember. This is a critical component in your conclusion. Never leave listeners wondering what your point was. Knowing that you'll be restating your message at the end encourages you to remain faithful to your mission throughout your sermon. This is not complex or difficult—just include a simple restatement of your message. You can easily weave this in with an introductory phrase of your own or one of the following:

"The one thing I want you to remember is . . . "
"It's clear from what we've learned today . . . "
"I join the prophet in encouraging you to . . . "
"In summary, it is apparent . . . "
"The pattern is plain throughout the scriptures . . . "

Close

Close by telling ward members exactly what you want them to do with the message you've given. Give them a call to action, a final commission. This is where you solidify what you want the audience to ponder, remember feel or act upon. People want to be motivated to take action. If the message is compelling, the action is more likely. Make the request gentle but clear.

The Savior gives a solid model in his final words recorded in the Gospel of Matthew, which represents the mission call for the Apostles: "Go ye therefore, and teach all nations, baptizing them in the name of the Father, and of the Son, and of the Holy Ghost: Teaching them to observe all things whatsoever I have commanded you: and, lo, I am with you always, even unto the end of the world. Amen" (MATTHEW 28:19–20).

Crafting an efficient but spiritually focused conclusion gives you the greatest chance to accomplish your stated mission. These three parts need to be woven together tightly for the greatest impact.

Your Spirit

Then he arose, and rebuked the wind . . .
and there was a calm.

Luke 8:24

A Testimony of the Task

Say to them that are of a fearful heart,
Be strong, fear not.

Isaiah 35:4

When the Lord gives you an assignment, He also makes it possible for the assignment to be completed. It would be comforting to receive a guarantee that the task would be risk-free and pain-free, but that's not the reality of this mortal probation. Just ask Nephi.

He probably thought after saying, "I will go and do," that a quick trip down to Jerusalem with his brothers would get those brass plates back from Laban and into father Lehi's hands. They asked politely. No results. They offered to buy them. No results. Nephi was then left with a totally unexpected and personally painful solution. But it required that Nephi find the courage to accomplish a difficult task—one that would make it possible to have the holy scriptures for the duration of their journey.

The clarity and extremity of the task required an inner conversation of significance and potency. This was no time for being wishy-washy. Nephi had to be strong, perhaps stronger than he had ever been before. He found strength in his spiritual conviction that what he was doing was the will of God.

The task of speaking in sacrament meeting, however unfamiliar and uncomfortable, is from the Lord. Don't whine—even to yourself. Find the strength to meet the challenge by gaining a spiritual confirmation that you have been chosen to deliver this message to ward members at this time for a sacred purpose, the fullness of which you may never know. We would do well to ask ourselves the question posed to Esther, "Who knoweth whether thou art come to the kingdom for such a time as this?" (ESTHER 4:14)

Prayer Brings Peace

Ye must not perform any thing unto the Lord
save in the first place
ye shall pray unto the Father in the name of Christ,
that he will consecrate thy performance.

2 Nephi 32:9

Up to the day you speak, most of your preparation is on paper. Suddenly, you find yourself seated on the stand, having left the world of the theoretical, where everything is perfect, for the far more uncomfortable world of reality, where nothing is perfect. The distance between what you want to accomplish and what you think you can accomplish looms as large as the Grand Canyon. The "butterflies" you feel are an indication that you know how important this occasion is—both for you and your audience. The Lord has every desire to bless you as you ask. Make prayer your partner in final preparation and your heart will be at peace.

Pray that you will do your best. This will relax you and boost your confidence. Then, after doing well, it will make it easier to face the challenge the next time. The Lord expects your best efforts. Don't twist that expectation into some unattainable model of perfect speaking. Your best will be sufficient as the Lord's abundant grace will attend you. "For we know that it is by grace that we are saved, after all we can do" (2 Nephi 25:23).

Pray that you will communicate His love. There are few things more important than sending the message of God's immense love for each person listening to you. If you ponder this in advance it will come out in your words and your voice. As you feel His love, you will find greater capacity to express it. "Beloved, let us love one another: for love is of God; and every one that loveth is born of God, and knoweth God" (1 JOHN 4:7).

Pray that you will sense the needs of the congregation. As you make final preparations, be thinking of modifications that might meet the unknown needs of those whom you are serving. Be open to inspiration that can direct where to look and how to express your ideas. The desire to have your sermon be a blessing is the motivation. "They did walk uprightly before God, imparting to one another both temporally and spiritually according to their needs and their wants" (MOSIAH 18:29).

Pray that your service will be consecrated. Alone, you cannot make your efforts holy; but the Lord can and will. You do not have to know in the end what purpose your words served as long as you place your work in his hands and speak with singleness of heart. "Faith, hope, charity and love, with an eye single to the glory of God, qualify [you] for the work" (D&C 4:5).

Pray that the Lord will bless you through the process. There are precious blessings—relationships, connections, opportunities, insights—unimagined and unsought that can come as a result of taking this process seriously. The Lord knows your needs and may be using this assignment to fulfill them. "Eye hath not seen, nor ear heard, neither have entered into the heart of man, the things which God hath prepared for them that love him" (1 CORINTHIANS 2:9).

Your prayers have the power to lead you to peace. Walk hand in hand with the Lord and He will bless you with unexpected joy.

Eliminate Self-Doubts

Remove from me reproach and contempt; for I have kept thy testimonies.

Psalm 119:22

Walking to junior high each morning required traversing a large dusty field of thistles, cactus and tumbleweeds. It also required crossing multiple unguarded railroad tracks. While scuffling through the field it was not uncommon to have a vicious prickly thorn from a *puncture weed* poke through the bottom of my thin-soled tennis shoes. Although it was tempting to limp along quickly to stay on schedule, I would always stop to remove the nasty prickle before crossing the railroad tracks. I didn't want anything to interfere with me getting across all the tracks without delay as I had heard what could happen to children who tripped and stumbled on the tracks. Crossing the tracks safely was my goal. Removing the thorn was a necessary part the process.

Removing the prickly burrs of self-doubt before beginning, opens up an immense array of positive possibilities. Before you start the process of writing, rehearsing and delivering a sermon, you must believe that you can do it.

Your effectiveness in sacrament meeting, to a large extent, is the result of your thoughts. Examine what you are thinking and saying so you can eliminate any thoughts that are negative. This will allow you to change the focus from your self-doubts to your desire to serve the Lord. Work at erasing these common negative thoughts.

"I can't believe I was asked to speak." Well, you were. The Lord believes in you. He has asked you to share a wonderful message with your brothers and sisters. Move ahead with courage and don't allow any self-doubt to delay your preparations. Procrastination can contribute to a self-fulfilling prophecy.

"I've never been a good speaker." No one is expecting perfection—just a positive message delivered with the Spirit. Prepare adequately and lovingly and you'll produce a message of value. Erase recollections of former negative experiences that continue to color your current self-perceptions. Start fresh and new with each opportunity.

"No one will take me seriously." The Lord does not fill the pulpit with gospel scholars every Sunday. Instead, He uses those who are on the front line in the battle of good versus evil. Your experience is more important than your eloquence. Speak from the heart.

Remember the insightful words of automaker, Henry Ford, "If you think you can do a thing or think you can't do a thing, you're right." Change your thinking and you change the outcome.

Do Not Fear Man

I will not fear what man shall do unto me.

Hebrews 13:6

Feeling nervous about speaking is so common that if you don't feel nervous, you're considered unusual. King Benjamin, who gave one of the most oft-quoted speeches in the scriptures, confessed his personal struggle regarding speaking to a gathering of that size: "For even at this time, my whole frame doth tremble exceedingly while attempting to speak unto you; but the Lord God doth support me, and hath suffered me that I should speak unto you" (Mosiah 2:30).

If the thought of speaking before fellow Saints makes you tremble, remember that you have that in common with one of the greatest speakers of all time.

You may want to ask yourself what is making you fearful. Answers typically fall into several broad categories.

- ✦ I'm afraid I'll forget what I was going to say (and I'll feel embarrassed)
- ✦ I'm afraid I'll say something stupid (and I'll feel embarrassed)

- ✦ I'm afraid that people won't like me or my message (and I'll feel embarrassed)
- ✦ I'm afraid I'll keep saying *um* (and I'll feel embarrassed)
- ✦ I'm afraid people will think I'm boring (and I'll feel embarrassed)
- ✦ I'm afraid people will think I'm a hypocrite (and I'll feel embarrassed)

Upon closer examination it's easy to see that it really boils down to one category—fear of humiliating yourself in front of people who know you. Unrealistic expectations generate anxiety. You are not called to astonish; you are called to preach. And your preaching is to be done in the name of the Lord. Remember whom you are serving.

President Ezra Taft Benson counseled, "The proud stand more in fear of men's judgment than of God's judgment. 'What will men think of me?' weighs heavier than 'What will God think of me?'"[1]

Pride is just as likely to make us fall silent as it is to cause us to boast. The Lord detailed that situation to the Saints in the summer of 1831. "But with some I am not well pleased, for they will not open their mouths, but they hide the talent which I have given unto them, because of the fear of man" (D&C 60:2). As you focus on your sermon as a consecrated gift to the Savior, you will feel strengthened.

Note

1. "Beware of Pride," *Ensign*, May 1989, 4.

Build Your Confidence

If ye are prepared ye shall not fear.

Doctrine and Covenants 38:30

A certain amount of anxiety is to be expected, and actually improves performance. Speaking professionals have known for years that complete calm, the absence of any internal flutters, actually impedes performance by diminishing energy. However, if past experience tells you that your nervousness will negatively impact your delivery, you may want to consider these five strategies: Prepare spiritually, rehearse sufficiently, organize completely, introduce and conclude powerfully, and speak to yourself positively.

Five Steps to Building Your Confidence

1. Prepare spiritually. Fasting, meditation and prayer during the preparation process assures you that you are creating a message that is pleasing to the Lord. When possible, a visit to the temple can open up additional avenues of personal revelation. Ask the Lord to strengthen you in His service. A priesthood blessing may be in order if you feel you need additional support.

2. Rehearse sufficiently. The purpose of rehearsing is to smooth out the rough spots so well that it will appear that you never needed any rehearsal at all. Don't be fooled into thinking that those who excel at the pulpit have not rehearsed. Depending on the level of discomfort you need to overcome, you may need to rehearse in front a mirror, rehearse before others and rehearse on-site. Don't expect that reading through your talk silently will be sufficient. Hearing yourself say the words you have planned will build your confidence.

3. Organize completely. Make certain that your sermon is logical and orderly in its organization. A predictable order of ideas will produce an additional level of comfort for you. Create notes that allow your ideas and words to flow. Well-prepared notes that are easy to read are essential.

4. Introduce and conclude powerfully. You can increase your confidence immensely by writing an engaging introduction and then rehearsing it well enough to give it without looking down. Starting off well gives you increased energy and most of your jitters will evaporate. You can find additional assurance in knowing you have a powerful and well-written conclusion to look forward to.

5. Speak to yourself positively. What you say to yourself as you prepare to speak really does matter. Develop positive affirmations which you can go over in your mind. You become the sum of your thoughts, so make them positive.

Before entering the chapel, you may want to have a final private word of prayer. Going into an unused classroom or even out to your car can give you the solitude to collect your thoughts and allow the Spirit to calm you.

Believe You Can Speak

Jesus said unto him,
If thou canst believe,
all things are possible to him that believeth.

Mark 9:23

At the nursery window, Peter Pan showed Wendy that all she needed in order to fly was to believe that she could fly. A simple change to make. Or was it? Even though the story of Peter Pan is a fanciful children's story, there is an important principle to learn.

The struggles many have with overcoming a fear of speaking in public can often be traced to a faulty belief system. Upgrade your belief system and you'll find ability to function without fear and talk without trembling.

Think about what you believe right now. If you believe that everyone is just waiting for you to make a mistake so they can point it out to you, then no wonder you're nervous. If you believe that you have to produce a word-perfect performance, you're setting yourself up for disaster. If you believe that your message is mundane and ward members could do just as well to stay home and read the *Ensign,* then you will lose your passion to perform. As a result of faulty thinking you send yourself counter-productive messages that tangle your tongue and muddle your mind. "The fear of man bringeth a snare: but whoso putteth his trust in the Lord shall be safe" (PROVERBS 29:25).

Before you ever step up to the pulpit, you must have firmly in your mind what it is that you're doing and whom you are serving. It's not a beauty pageant, job interview or political rally. It's sacrament meeting. You are on an errand from the Lord.

Believe something more powerful. An adjustment of your thinking is like a needed course correction mid-flight. It may seem minor, but you'll never arrive without it. These affirmations emphasize the value of what you've been called to do. You may want to post these phrases someplace visited daily (mirror, refrigerator, steering wheel, etc.). Perhaps a 3" x 5" card in your scriptures would help. Read your affirmations out loud. They are most effective when you hear your own voice expressing them. If you feel doubt creeping in, pray that the Lord will reinforce their validity in your heart.

1. The Lord has asked me to speak for His own purpose
2. Members of my ward want me to succeed
3. I have prepared sufficiently to succeed
4. Members of my ward will be blessed by the message I have prepared

You may have other affirmations that you find helpful. Keep them brief and honest. Recite them aloud until your mind, body and spirit agree. Eventually they will feel authentic. As soon as you've amended your belief system, you're ready to move forward and speak with confidence.

Dress for the Occasion

Man looketh on the outward appearance,
but the Lord looketh on the heart.

1 Samuel 16:7

The Lord explained to Samuel how fruitless it is to make judgments based on how someone looks. Yet, the reality is that we do it every day. Since childhood we've been told that you can't judge a book by its cover, but we do it anyway. The manner in which you dress can contribute to the calm you seek before speaking when you know it's in harmony with the teachings of the Lord.

What is essential for speaking in sacrament meeting is clothing that will not detract from the message. It's a simple requirement—but one that is difficult to deal with just before Church on Sunday morning. It takes some planning. Ideally, your goal is to match the formality of the presiding authority at sacrament meeting. Some cultural traditions may influence what you choose to wear. You need to be both sensitive and flexible, as styles and expectations do evolve over time. There have been more than a few changes in dress since the Church was organized in 1830. But the objective is to project an image of reverence, modesty and respect.

Regarding dress for any situation, the young people of the Church have been counseled in *For the Strength of Youth*, "The way you dress is a reflection of what you are on the inside. Your dress and grooming send messages about you to others and influence the way you and others act."[1] The principle is universal and applies to us all.

Below are a few simple guidelines that may get you started on selecting clothes appropriate for speaking in sacrament meeting.

Brethren

For the brethren, the pattern is established clearly the first time you pass the sacrament: white shirt and tie. But as a speaker is there more? Even in summer, a long-sleeved shirt appears more respectful. Your shirt should be clean and pressed the night before. The tie should be traditional, but not necessarily dark. Make sure there is not a spot on your tie. Avoid high fashion ties with commercial characters or designs that can be distracting. Dark slacks are best with dark socks in a similar tone. A dark, conservative jacket or suit, when available, is a nice touch for communicating a reverent feeling. Polishing your shoes can give you extra confidence.

Sisters

For the sisters, the issues are a bit more complex. A long-sleeved blouse and skirt or long-sleeved dress or suit is ideal. Modesty is essential, but may need to be checked by someone else before you walk out the door. The length of the skirt or the height of a slit can be problematic. Also check the neckline. A difficulty with some current styles is the sheerness or clinging nature of the fabric. You can sometimes go with brighter colors, but solids will always communicate more reverence than patterns or prints. Avoid distracting jewelry or accessories. Closed-toe shoes are considered more formal than sandals. If you plan to wear stockings, check for problems while a remedy is still possible.

Reduce Stress

For both brethren and sisters, the key is planning. You should not feel compelled to purchase a new outfit; being clean and looking your best is all that is expected. Select what you will wear the night before so you can sleep well, knowing all is in readiness.

The message you're delivering should be the central focus of the listeners' attention. The Lord already considers you wonderful and splendid, just the way you are. Simplicity will make your message the focal point.

Note

1. *For the Strength of Youth* (2001), 14–15.

Don't Point Out Your Faults

And Moses went and spake these words . . .
I am an hundred and twenty years old this day;
I can no more go out and come in.

Deuteronomy 31:1–2

Can you imagine this situation? You climb aboard a jet, ready for the vacation of a lifetime. Soon after take off, the pilot comes on the intercom and announces the following: "I know you won't believe this, but this is my very first flight. So please forgive me if the trip's a little bit bumpy. I thought I did pretty well on the takeoff, but I was sure nervous when the plane left the runway. I couldn't tell if we were gonna make it. But we did. So hang on and I'll let you know if I have any more problems during the flight." You'd never hear something like that if the pilot plans on remaining employed. Why? Because it causes every person on the flight to have doubts that they'll ever make it to the final destination.

The situation is familiar. Feelings of inadequacy sweep over you and almost unexpectedly the words come tumbling out:

"Forgive me, I have a sore throat . . . "
"I don't know very much about this topic . . . "
"This probably isn't going to be very good . . . "

" I can't believe I forgot I was speaking today . . . "
"I hope you can't see how much I'm shaking . . . "
"You're probably wondering why they would ask me . . . "
"I've never been very good at this . . . "
"I only found out about this assignment last night . . . "
"You certainly know more about this than I do . . . "
"I couldn't believe it when the bishop asked me . . . "
"I am so nervous . . . "
"I hope you'll bear with me as I try to get through this . . . "

Two reasons to stop. First of all, as you accidentally let phrases like these spill out, you cause the entire ward to wonder if they'll ever make it to the "final destination." Stop and think. Is there a final destination—a sacred place filled with new spiritual understanding and valuable knowledge—that you want to take them to? Then let them know that, and then do everything in your power to get them there safely. Don't give them any reason to think that something might happen along the way—this gives members of the ward permission to tune out. And that's the last thing you want to do.

Second, this puts the focus on you rather than your listeners. Avoid any behaviors that draw attention to you and detour you from your final destination. A successful journey, no matter how bumpy, must remain the focus.

Ward members want to make the voyage with you and arrive safe and sound. Give them every reason to look forward to the trip.

Get a Good Night's Rest

Retire to thy bed early, that ye may not be weary; arise early, that your bodies and your minds may be invigorated.

Doctrine and Covenants 88:124

It is not uncommon to request of the Lord the blessing of a "good night's rest" as you conclude a busy day. This is not unreasonable if requested early enough in the evening to make it possible. Sometimes the request is actually for a "miracle," when too few hours remain between setting your head on your pillow and jumping back up in the morning.

This is especially critical on the day of speaking in sacrament meeting. Mismanaging the amount of time it takes to create a meaningful message can leave a speaker with a late night session just putting pen to paper. Add to this the time required to edit, rewrite and rehearse and you could see the first glimmers of dawn before your presentation is polished.

The dilemma created at this point is that your mental machinery will be "gummed up" as a result of insufficient rest. Being able to recall memorized passages or the details of a spiritually stirring anecdote may be impossible. Your enunciation may be compromised and your facial expressions subdued. Your ability to speed up or slow down at precisely the right moment may be off and your vocal inflections are likely to be muddled or mistimed. Even your ability to read can be affected. A perfectly splendid talk may be washed down the drain due to lack of sleep.

Planning ahead may decrease the probability of landing in a time crunch and increase the probability of getting enough sleep on Saturday night. Here is a reasonable timetable assuming you are given two weeks to prepare. If you are have less time, condense the schedule. Do not underestimate the time required to create and rehearse an inspiring sermon. Proper time management will help allow for that good night's rest you're looking for.

14 days	Get date/topic/details from Bishopric/start study
10 days	Finish narrowing/select mission/message
7 days	Complete first draft/first rehearsal aloud/edit
4 days	Final draft/multiple rehearsals/check timing
2 days	Work on memorizing portions/polish delivery
1 day	Final rehearsals/develop conversational tone

Deliver
with Power

Have I no power to deliver?

Isaiah 50:2

Use Your Whole Body

Let thy heart be of good cheer before my face;
and thou shalt bear record of my name . . .
and thou shalt send forth my word unto the ends of the earth.

Doctrine and Covenants 112:4

Cell phones are today's modern marvel in communication. You can call anyone from anywhere. But cell phones are not without their limitations and frustrations. It seems like whenever someone is giving you critical information, like complicated directions or an address, the call starts breaking up. Or another call comes in. Or there's static. Or the battery goes dead. So much for infallible technology. As splendid as cell phones are, they are still imperfect in delivering information. But so are we.

Even when the message you have prepared on paper seems perfect, the unknown factor is how the message will come across once you stand at the podium and begin speaking. Delivery is an art; in the case of speaking in sacrament meeting, an *inspired* art form. Every person who delivers a sermon does so differently, imprinting their personality on the process.

As a speaker it is imperative that you do everything you can to make the message come through loud and clear. Although delivery does not demand perfection, communication is enhanced through two layers of understanding. First, learn which behaviors fortify your effectiveness. Develop those skills. Second, learn which behaviors sabotage your effectiveness. Eliminate those as completely as possible. Scrutinize your speaking style and then remove any static or interference that you are creating through your own disruptive mannerisms or habits.

Body. Discover how posture, podium approach, and body movement can communicate positive or negative attitudes.

Hands. Learn how to gesture effectively and how to keep your hands out of trouble.

Voice. Remove annoying filler words and use your voice expressively by varying your rate, pitch, volume, and pauses.

Face. Facial expressions, especially a warm smile, can help you connect with your audience.

Eyes. Work at developing good eye contact with your audience.

As you become aware of how your body contributes or detracts from your message, you can make the minor adjustments that will strengthen your presentation style. Rehearsal will allow you to upgrade your non-verbal communication so that it is harmonious with the content and tone of your sermon.

Eye Contact

They shall see eye to eye,
when the Lord shall bring again Zion.

Isaiah 52:8

One of the most essential practices of a speaker is making a personal connection with listeners through eye contact. The term is widely used but rarely completely understood. It doesn't mean just glancing around the room, staring at one person or deliberately staring over the heads of ward members. These would not accomplish the goal of connecting with your entire audience.

Eye contact is a skill that is developed incrementally, once basic principles are understood.

Be familiar with your text. The more secure you are with the text of your talk, the more easily you can look up and connect. When you are totally dependent on the printed word, you lose the flexibility to speak from the heart. As you rehearse, keep the goal of building eye contact in mind.

Smile with your eyes and your mouth. Part of the relationship-building process that occurs when you speak takes place through the warmth of your eyes and smile. Without a smile, eye contact can feel threatening. A genuine smile breaks down any barriers. Once the audience decides they can trust you—something that is often based more on non-verbal cues than on actual words spoken—you can be assured your message will sink more deeply into their hearts.

Look directly into the faces of specific people. Please ignore the advice occasionally given to look out over the heads of people to make it seem like you're having eye contact. It doesn't work for you or your audience. Instead, look right into the eyes and faces of a variety of people. If you need to, you can arrange in advance who will look back at you and smile.

Connect until you finish a sentence or thought. You will probably find it ineffective to connect for a set amount of time. It will feel more natural to stay with each person long enough to finish a sentence or compete a thought. As you glance down at your notes, it will be easy to change to a different part of the room.

Connect with all areas of the chapel. Even though your family or best friend may be seated on the front row, find a friendly face in each section of the room. Your eye contact connects everyone to your message and also connects everyone to each other. Don't overlook the far sides and deep into the back. Everyone needs to feel included.

As your confidence increases, you will begin to focus on the needs of your audience and sense the importance of eye contact to them.

Managing the Microphone

When Abraham's servant heard their words,
he worshipped the Lord.

Genesis 24:52

"Can you hear me now?" The tagline from one of the most annoying commercials in history makes a serious point. People need to hear you. They want to hear you. Until they *can* hear you, no communication takes place. It is up to you to make certain you can be heard. But staring you right in the face is a threatening and intimidating piece of modern electronic wizardry: The microphone.

It should be simple to step up to the microphone and speak. However, unless you speak often, you may be a bit uncomfortable with speaking into a microphone. It is somewhat unnerving to hear your magnified voice resounding throughout the chapel. Given the size and design of most meetinghouses today, microphones are a necessity. Adjusting your attitude is the only option. Getting accustomed to using a microphone will increase your ability to speak in a relaxed manner.

Becoming proficient at the microphone is a matter of a few simple steps and multiple trips to the podium. Each time it should become a little easier.

Until it is as smooth as silk, you may find the following ideas helpful. Some suggestions are for before you speak, to help you feel comfortable with the sound of your own voice and the workings of the microphone. Some suggestions are for when you actually stand to speak.

Before You Speak:

1. Test the sensitivity and volume of the microphone before the day you speak.
2. If testing on a Sunday, be sure the room is mostly empty; do not test while the chapel is filling or prelude or postlude music is playing.
3. Do not scratch or tap on the microphone, just say, "Check, check" in your normal speaking voice. This will help you get a feel for how sensitive the microphone is.
4. Determine a comfortable distance from your mouth. It will normally be 6–8", but check it out by taking someone with you.
5. Check for necessary voice volume for the entire chapel by having friends or family sit in different seats in the chapel.
6. If possible, give a portion of your sermon in advance so you can increase your comfort level.

When You Speak:

1. Make sure the microphone is powered on. You can't always tell in a crowded room.
2. If a member of the bishopric doesn't raise the pulpit high enough, glance back and motion to him to move it up before you begin speaking.
3. Tip the microphone head toward you so it doesn't cover your face and is in the best position to pick up your voice.
4. Once in place, don't readjust the microphone during your sermon.
5. Properly positioned, there should be no need to lean into the microphone. Stand completely upright and relaxed.

6. Be careful not to bump the microphone while gesturing or to knock it with your scriptures when placing them on the pulpit.

Your goal is to make the message you have prepared audible to everyone in the chapel. Only when it is heard, can the members respond. When prepared to use the microphone you will never have to ask if you can be heard—instead you will proclaim, "Hear me, and hearken to the word of the Lord" (JACOB 2:27).

Speak to Be Heard

Let every man be swift to hear, slow to speak.

James 1:19

Everyone in your ward wants to easily understand what you have to say. This means developing a "public speaking voice." You will speak more slowly, more clearly and more expressively than you would in normal conversation, while still maintaining a conversational tone. At first it will seem forced and awkward, but eventually you will realize that this is what it takes for your message to be communicated. Will the skill come quickly and easily? Possibly not. It will take concerted effort and multiple sessions of practice to master this new style of speaking.

Slowly. It's easy to get so excited by what you have to say that you rush right through it. Slow down so that everyone can capture your words and your ideas. Even after you try slowing it down on your first practice, you may need to slow it down even further. Don't confuse slowing it down with making it drag. You still need to maintain a level of energy and enthusiasm.

Clearly. As a culture, we have gotten increasingly sloppy in our enunciation and articulation. This may sound like something for which your grandmother would have scolded you. But the truth is that you multiply the chances of being understood by carefully pronouncing each word. You don't want to make it sound unnatural, but if you slur your words, it becomes easy for those listening to mistake one word for another and then miss the point you were trying to make. Working toward clearer articulation takes practice. Good examples can be found at general conference.

Expressively. To pass the flame from your heart to the hearts of ward members, you must learn to speak expressively. This comes naturally to all of us. When? In conversations one-on-one. Just think of the last time you spoke of a new baby, a favorite sports team, frightening accident or a hilarious movie. The human voice is naturally animated. For some reason, when approaching the podium, the ability to speak expressively flies out the window. When a monotonous voice that neither rises nor falls takes over, the message sounds like the dull drip of a distant faucet instead of the highly energized message of inspiration that you had prepared. Developing a fully animated voice takes committed practice.

Think of the Savior on the Mount of Beatitudes. His sermon was so powerful and memorable that it is still quoted 2000 years later. Imagine the speed, clarity and expression that He used in sharing those sacred principles in order to be sure that everyone remembered them.

Paint with Your Voice

For if the trumpet give an uncertain sound,
who shall prepare himself to the battle?

1 Corinthians 14:8

If a painter uses canvas and paint, what does a speaker use? The voice. A tiny body part that emits custom-made sound waves on command. A miracle, really. Your voice is how you communicate your message. Using a variation of vocal sound will multiply your effectiveness as a speaker.

Volume. Make sure you can be heard in all areas of chapel. Vary your volume as needed for expression. Avoid whispering or speaking too softly for long periods as it fatigues listeners. Too loud can seem intimidating or rude. No one wants to be shouted at.

Pace. The speed at which you speak can add a feeling of urgency (by speeding up) or underscore importance (by slowing down). Try different pacing at various parts of your talk to add clarity. Develop a pace that will draw people in, not put them to sleep. If you're feeling nervous, be careful not to rush.

Pitch. Use more of the vocal range of your voice. Dropping your voice slightly is one method to clarify when a quote is being given. Varying the pitch is a natural part of interpersonal communication and needs to be expanded when speaking from the pulpit.

Emphasis. Stressing a particular word or phrase makes it easier for listeners to hear what you want them to notice. This is especially helpful when reading a passage of scripture. The audience appreciates being able to tell what you feel deserves to be emphasized.

Pause. A well-placed pause can add a touch of drama and suspense in a story. Don't be afraid of silence that is deliberately included.

Eliminate vocalized pauses. Avoid filling space with *um, er* or *uh*. If this is something you wrestle with, practice with audio or video until you smooth out your delivery. A brief unintended pause is better than a filler word.

Magnetic vocal delivery. This skill will be the result of using all the elements of vocal variety. It will require practice in front of a live audience and discovering the best way to use your voice to accomplish your objective. Over time you will develop a warm conversational style with expressive qualities—just what the audience wants to hear.

Loud and Soft

It was a still voice of perfect mildness,
as if it had been a whisper,
and it did pierce even to the very soul.

Helaman 5:30

It is easy to assume that only a loud voice is heard and taken seriously. Actually one of the softest voices among all the modern prophets—President Kimball's—was taken very seriously. His messages resonated across the globe and he is still widely quoted today.

If you are a naturally soft-spoken person, explore using a louder version of your voice for key points, but don't strain or sound screechy. Test with your family and get accurate feedback. If you tend to be a bit on the loud side, work at developing a more gentle voice. Developing the dynamic range of your voice, allows stories, quotations and personal experiences to be expressed more dramatically. Experiment as you rehearse and discover how just changing the volume can make a difference.

When might you speak more loudly? When you are quoting the Lord or one of His prophets commanding or chastising, you may want to increase the volume. If in a story, there is something frightening or alarming, you may want to emphasize it. In your conclusion, you may want to underscore your testimony by increasing your volume just a notch.

When might you speak more softly? When quoting a particularly tender passage of scripture or poetry you may want to soften the volume a bit. When telling a personal story and you reach the portion where you are faced with a dilemma, you can step outside the story for a moment and speak in a softer voice to discuss the options you were considering.

Develop your own personal style that magnifies the meaning of your message for the congregation. "Let all those that put their trust in thee rejoice: let them ever shout for joy" (PSALM 5:11).

Avoid Filler Words

Except ye utter by the tongue words easy to be understood, how shall it be known what is spoken? For ye shall speak into the air.

1 Corinthians 14:9

If you've ever been in a car with a brand new driver, you know the feeling of whiplash caused by the erratic stopping and starting that comes from not knowing the gas pedal from the brake pedal. With practice, the driver eventually learns the controls and smooths out their driving style.

In much the same way you can smooth out your speaking style by removing unnecessary filler words. As you do so, you'll be blessed with increased confidence and effectiveness. Filler words, also known as vocalized pauses, interrupt your train of thought—in fact the train can be completely derailed. Remove the words and you'll stay on track.

A slight pause or brief silence, nestled between thoughts, is rarely noticed by listeners. Whereas a vocalized pause, the dreadful *um,* often stands out as a glaringly misplaced sound. It does nothing to contribute to the message and diminishes your credibility. Get accustomed to the sound of silence. A pause can actually add a touch of drama when placed with care.

Correcting this in your speaking style takes conscious effort and practice. If any of the following words or sounds have been heard more than a few times in a talk you've given, you may want to develop a strategy to remove them from future talks. A good friend or family member may be the best coach on the extraction of these potentially annoying sounds. They are generally a habitual addition—something of which you are unaware—that someone else will have to assist you in overcoming. Once you become aware of where you normally place them, you can, with effort, replace them with sweet, blessed silence as you move to your next point. Your message will be more memorable and you will become more confident.

Watch for these common filler words:

"Um"
"Uh"
"Er"
"OK"
"Yunno"
"All right . . . "
"Like"
"Well . . . "
"Let's see now . . . "
"And then . . . "
"So . . . "

Your message will come across with greater impact without the diluting effect of these unwelcome and meaningless sounds. Work on overcoming this habit, but don't berate yourself if it takes some time.

USE YOUR HANDS

Let your hands be strengthened,
and be ye valiant.

2 SAMUEL 2:7

MOSES UNDERSTOOD THE VALUE of using his hands. When his hands were raised, the Israelites triumphed in battle. When his hands came down, they lost. He even brought in Aaron and Hur to help him keep his hands aloft. "And it came to pass, when Moses held up his hand, that Israel prevailed: and when he let down his hand, Amalek prevailed" (EXODUS 17:11).

In spite of this valuable role model, most of us keep our hands very still while speaking—almost as if using them will disturb the peace and disrupt the sermon. Appropriate gesturing adds emphasis and accent when needed. President Hinckley is not afraid to use his hands while speaking. In fact, his chopping gesture has an almost "signature" quality to it. The Saints know when he is mentioning something he feels strongly about.

So, you may want to take those hands out of your pockets and off the podium. When it's time to emphasize a point, you need to have your hands ready to go to work. Keep in mind that not everything you do with your hands is helpful.

There are a few things you want to avoid while at the podium in order to keep the focus on your message:

Both hands in pockets (one is generally all right)
Jingling coins or keys
Hand wringing
Hands or elbows glued to sides
Hands on hips
Grasping both sides of podium
Hands tightly folded
Arms folded across chest
Clenched fists
Finger pointing
Random gestures
Clapping for no reason
Scratching anywhere
Touching face or hair

Chances are you don't even realize you are doing these unless someone else points it out. Once you become aware, you need to replace your habits with positive hand movement. It can be minimal, but still needs to be thought about.

You may want to try the *ready-to-speak* position. Try it without a podium to get the feel. With your arms relaxed, bend your elbows at about 90° and keep them slightly away from your body. Your forearms are held out in an open position, with your hands relaxed and nearly vertical. This communicates honesty, energy and vulnerability to your audience and leaves you ready to make appropriate use of your hands for emphasis through gestures. You can drop one hand to the podium to rest on your notes, using the other hand to gesture. Switching off will allow you to gesture with either hand. If this is too uncomfortable, consider gently resting your hands on the podium. This leaves them high enough to gesture should you choose to do so.

You may find it helpful to rehearse a few specific well-timed and suitable gestures for your most important points. Work on form and timing. Try them out in front of a mirror to make sure the gestures are high enough and bold enough to be noticed. Feedback from others will be essential to give you enough confidence to follow through. You are guaranteed to feel awkward and ridiculous to begin with. Know that all speakers gesture to some degree, even if it is only subtly.

As you add gestures to your non-verbal vocabulary, you will find yourself getting more comfortable. Almost every painting of Jesus speaking shows him gesturing boldly. It is part of the language of public speaking.

Learn to Gesture

And his chains fell off from his hands.

Acts 12:7

When facing an audience, your hands can feel like dead weights at the end of your arms. If nerves take over, it feels like the only choices are to grab the pulpit, stick them in your pockets or drape them at your sides. These uncooperative pesky appendages can follow commands once properly trained. Ideally, the gestures you use will flow from the passion already in your text and in your heart.

The good news is that in normal conversation you already gesture effectively and frequently. To develop your capacity to gesture effectively at the podium requires experimentation and practice. Try this exercise and you will be convinced that you can add gestures to your next sacrament meeting talk. The exercise is entertaining and will reveal your native capacity for gesturing.

Gesture Development Exercise

1. Read through each of these phrases in an expressive voice. Imagine the hand gesture that would naturally be connected with that part of a story or point.

2. Try saying the line with a gesture. Try a couple of different gestures. Repeat the gesture until the timing is right and it feels comfortable.

3. Do it front of a mirror. You may want to add facial expressions that seem appropriate.

"He held a tiny bird in his hands . . . "
"He covered his face in shame . . . "
"She picked up the dead mouse . . . "
"He straightened his tie . . . "
"She tossed his book on the ground . . . "
"He rubbed his cold hands in front of the fire . . . "
"She pointed toward the exit . . . "
"The fish was at least this big . . . "
"He pulled back the curtains and looked outside . . . "
"Suddenly, a bright light flashed . . . "
"In this book are eternal truths . . . "
"She brushed the confetti off her dress . . . "
"He covered his ears before the bomb exploded . . . "
"She wiped a tear from her eye . . . "
"He crossed his arms and waited for the real story . . . "
"There are three ways to accomplish this . . . "
"There is nothing more valuable than this . . . "
"Just outside there is a world awaiting your testimony . . . "

Now try saying the lines with no movement at all. If you had a good experience with this, then you will recognize the value and emphasis gestures can add when you speak in sacrament meeting. Until gesturing at the pulpit becomes fluid for you, it will take commitment and practice. Remember, the point is not to become overly theatrical, but to make your message more meaningful and engaging for those who listen.

Your Body Matters

If, therefore, thine eye be single,
thy whole body shall be full of light.

3 Nephi 13:22

When you're at the grocery store and are about to purchase a small non-grocery item, does the packaging really matter to you? If there are only two left and one has a torn wrapper and one is perfectly whole, which one do you choose? If you're like most folks, you'll choose the one that has the perfect packaging. For whatever reason, the packaging of the product matters.

While busily constructing a thoughtful sermon, you may not have given much thought to what role your body plays in delivering your ideas. Non-verbal communication—everything from tone of voice to where you put your hands—is responsible for over half of the message that is received. It's the human packaging.

When your words don't match your body language, the audience is always more inclined to believe the non-verbal cues. Just consider your reaction if someone with a grimace, slouch and sour voice claimed to be "so grateful to speak to you."

Align your body with your message and you have the added power of whole body communication. How you face the audience and how you stand may seem to be small details, but it communicates subtly to the audience how much you care. Your goal is to be simultaneously relaxed and energetic.

You can do this by placing yourself directly in front of the pulpit, standing up straight, shoulders back, looking out into the audience, feet about a foot apart, and knees slightly bent. If you don't plan in advance, you could find some of the following negative and distracting body habits interrupting your well-planned sermon.

Body Stance Habits to Eliminate

- Too stiff
- Feet too far apart
- Slouching on podium
- Turning to one side of chapel only
- Visibly shifting weight back and forth
- Leaning to one side
- Being hunched over

Body Movement Habits to Eliminate

- Flamingo position (standing on one leg)
- Going on tippy-toes
- Rocking back and forth
- Bouncing up and down
- Approaching podium too quickly or awkwardly
- Leaving podium too quickly or awkwardly
- Turning to speak to those behind you

The way you stand and move communicates your preparation, state-of-mind, testimony, and attitude toward the opportunity to speak. Make sure your body is giving the same message your words are. Exude warmth and confidence by standing straight and tall and avoiding unnecessary or nervous movement. Your body will communicate that you are relaxed and prepared. This will multiply the impact of your message.

ABANDON NERVOUS HABITS

Then would I speak, and not fear.

JOB 9:35

IN THE FLOWER GARDEN IN MY FRONT YARD I carefully removed every emerging oak sapling that was even thinking about taking up residence. I was assured that the 2½ feet of topsoil shoveled over the top would keep any runners from nearby oak trees from surfacing. Confident, I planted tulips, iris, petunias, dahlias and daffodils. I relaxed and celebrated my victory over nature.

My celebration was brief. Much like bad habits that seem to resurface with no difficulty, I now find myself plucking oak saplings from my garden on a weekly basis.

To be an effective speaker, getting nervous habits under control is essential—but it's not a one-time weeding, it's more of a maintenance project. Just as I can now identify a baby oak tree as soon as it breaks the surface of my garden soil, you need to be able to identify nervous habits that you want to control the moment they show up in a sermon.

Keep in mind that none of these habits will destroy your sermon, but they will erode your credibility and distract your audience from focusing on your message.

Vocalized pauses such as *um*
Clearing throat
Chewing gum
Playing with tie
Fiddling with rings
Dragging fingers through hair
Rubbing nose
Touching face
Drumming fingers on podium
Excessive handling of notes/note cards
Playing with or chewing on pen/pencil
Pushing hair behind ear
Clicking or tapping pen
Buttoning and unbuttoning coat
Playing with microphone
Pushing glasses up nose
Tugging at clothes
Scratching head or other places
Sniffling (quietly use tissue, please)
Checking watch or clock
Grating teeth
Neglecting to breathe normally

This list is not exhaustive, so you may have one that doesn't appear here. Usually speakers will only have one or two nervous habits to contend with. But because these habits are so ingrained, you may be completely oblivious to them. Practicing with video or with an audience is a good way to become aware of them and develop a strategy for keeping them in check. You may never remove them permanently or completely, but if you can diminish their visibility, your delivery will be more confident and effective.

Speak with Enthusiasm

Therefore, dearly beloved brethren,
let us cheerfully do all things that lie in our power.

Doctrine and Covenants 123:17

Most of us use the word "enthusiasm" regularly to describe the bubbly, effervescent and energetic personalities of some people we know. A little research reveals that the meaning of enthusiasm goes much deeper than a simple personality trait—it is a deep yearning of the spirit that is manifest in how we communicate. It means to "have God within us." A sacred transformation that signifies a change from within.

God's most important work is accomplished by those of us who are "anxiously engaged" and delivering his message with energy. President Spencer W. Kimball explained, "Enthusiasm is real interest plus dedicated energy, and this combination provides the most dynamic of all human qualities. But anyone who does not have it naturally can cultivate it."[1] So how do you communicate with enthusiasm?

Approach. Step right up to the podium like you belong there.

Posture. Stand up straight and tall. Your mother was right. No slouching.

Face. A beaming smile, when consistent with your message, energizes you and the recipients.

Voice. Use a strong and expressive voice. No need to shout, but speak as if you mean it.

Close. Conclude with conviction. You will never have an opportunity to give this talk to these people ever again. Etch your message upon their hearts. Make certain that the audience feels that you've preached the "good news" of the gospel.

President Kimball, known as a bundle of enthusiasm himself, observed, "You can speak a very mediocre sermon and do it with enthusiasm and people will think it was great. You can give a most profound sermon on a monotone basis and people may go to sleep, and they may say, that was the driest man I ever heard. Actually, it was profound. . . . Give it with enthusiasm and make them know you believe it."[2]

Perhaps it would be wise to take the counsel of Alexis de Tocqueville who observed that Christian pulpits should be "ablaze with righteousness."[3] That certainly matches the message of the hymn, "The Spirit of God Like a Fire Is Burning," with lyrics that summon up images of the most powerful and blazing angelic ministrations.

Enthusiasm, a quality of spiritual zeal that can be passed on to others, occurs when individual members called to speak bring spiritual energy to the pulpit. Enthusiasm is a gift of the Spirit which can be sought by anyone. It should naturally attend those who are possessed of the Holy Spirit. Allow your enthusiasm to come to the surface. When it is present, it blesses and inspires both the speaker and the listeners.

Notes

24. *The Teachings of Spencer W. Kimball*, ed. Edward L. Kimball (1982), 573.
25. Ibid.
26. *Democracy in America* (1835).

Develop a Friendly Style

And the Lord spake unto Moses face to face, as a man speaketh unto his friend.

Exodus 33:11

You'll be more at ease at the pulpit if you develop a warm, conversational style—like speaking to a friend. The audience feels the same way. It is comfortable to be addressed by someone who likes you and wants what is best for you. Of course, your friendliness needs to be a permanent part of your personality, not something you slip on like a jacket as you approach the podium. "A friend loveth at all times" (Proverbs 17:17), but the stress of speaking can sometimes make your natural affability and warmth less visible. Bring it to the surface.

One who has developed this to near-perfection is President Gordon B. Hinckley. His congenial style has even surprised the prickliest of media interviewers. His consistent warmth shows his genuine concern for the well-being of all of Heavenly Father's children. This is a model that we would be wise to emulate.

There are three components to a friendly style: tone of voice, word selection and delivery style. All of them are fueled by the "pure love of Christ."

Tone of voice. Develop a tone that is warm and loving, not condemning. Even when delivering sobering words on a difficult topic, your tone of voice can express tenderness and concern. Jacob did that well with one of the toughest sermons recorded in the Book of Mormon.

Word selection. Select common and uplifting words, ones that have a conversational feel to them. At the same time, in order to show reverence, you'll want to avoid slang terms. Be careful of using overly academic or high-minded terminology. Most gospel discussions at the pulpit are application oriented, so you'll want to work toward sharing your experiences with the gospel in action.

Delivery style. Think of an animated conversation with your best friend concerning good news. If you use that as your pattern, you should be full of optimism and enthusiasm. When talking with your friends you don't read from notes—you speak from the heart. Eyes are "windows to the soul," so give lots of eye contact.

Don't confuse a friendly style with a style that is overly casual or informal. People will listen to those who communicate friendliness, rather than formal stiffness and stuffiness. But there is still a reverence that must be maintained when speaking in the name of the Lord.

Rehearse Your Message

I did rehearse unto them the words of Isaiah.

1 Nephi 15:20

When you don't speak often, you can easily be under the impression that rehearsing somehow removes the spontaneity and warmth of a message. The opposite is actually true. When the sermon is insufficiently rehearsed, you are more likely to be stiff, anxious and insecure.

Rehearsing does not mean that you will automatically improve. In fact, ineffective rehearsals can actually increase your anxiety by making you more aware of your inadequacies with no strategy to improve.

Set aside time for prayerful practice sessions. Before you begin, create the best set of notes or manuscript from which to rehearse. Then read or speak out loud so that the process of improvement can begin.

What to Do

Find a quiet place to rehearse. You will want your first rehearsals to be uninterrupted and in private. There's much to be worked through on the first draft. Don't just whisper your talk or rehearse it in your mind. Speak right up.

Watch for problem words or phrases. Catch any unruly tongue twisters or awkward phrases. Make sure that what you wrote down is what you're actually saying. There's only one letter difference between *immorality* and *immortality*, but there's a world of difference in meaning.

Rewrite as necessary. Don't think of your outline or manuscript as being cast in concrete once you have your first draft finished. Speaking out loud will generate valuable revisions. Note anything you think might need to be rewritten as soon as you realize a change is necessary. If you just continue rehearsing, you'll probably forget.

Modify notes. You may find you need to remind yourself to say a word with greater emphasis or slow down for a certain passage. Jot that down in your notes.

Work on expression. Practice sharing your ideas expressively. It may sound funny to you at first, but you need to be just a bit more expressive than you would be in a normal conversation. Practice until that feels comfortable.

Commit important sections to memory. The more you have *almost* memorized, the more you can look up and connect with the audience. It doesn't need to be word perfect. You just want a fluid, relaxed version each time you practice. Having the introduction and conclusion down cold allows for maximum contact and expression. Those are two sections that really need your attention. You'll be glad if you know them well.

Work on finding and reading scriptures. Scripture passages can be a real challenge—from finding the right page to working through archaic sentence structure. Smooth it all out through practice. Make sure you know the meaning of unfamiliar words.

What to Use

Use audio tape or digital recorder. Hearing your voice will allow you to become aware of vocalized pauses, which are the addition of filler words like *um* and *er*. Adjust your delivery to remove them. Become accustomed to periodic silence. You will also notice if your voice needs greater expression.

Use a mirror. This will give you a chance to see your facial expressions, posture and gestures. It's helpful, but not as valuable as video.

Use video. If someone can videotape your practice, you can begin to see mannerisms that may get in the way of communicating. You can also polish gestures that will enhance your message.

Speak before a real audience. Gathering a few friends or family can be helpful to identify any places where your message gets muddled or confusing. You usually cannot find these yourself, even with video.

Use a mock pulpit. Create a practice pulpit with boxes or lumber. This can help you become more confident in how you'll use the space and manage your notes and the scriptures.

Use the real pulpit. You may need to practice at the pulpit from which you'll be speaking. Talk to the priesthood leader who invited you to see what arrangements need to be made to access the chapel.

Blessings Which Come to You

There is an amazing array of blessings that will come to you as a result of taking the time to seriously rehearse. First of all, you will be more relaxed as you speak. Second, you will be more connected to the audience. Third, your message will come across more clearly. And finally, the message you practice thoroughly will be engraved upon your heart so you'll remember it forever.

Gospel Grown-Ups

When I was a child, I spake as a child . . .
but when I became a man, I put away childish things.

1 Corinthians 13:11

The days of excusing a missing homework assignment by blaming it on the dog are behind you. But some of us still struggle with making excuses when we stand up to speak. Speak as a mature member of God's kingdom regardless of any doubts you have about your native talents in public speaking. Your maturity in the gospel will shine through.

It is tempting to think that ward members will excuse an ill-prepared sermon if you explain to them why it is impossible for you to give one. In actuality, you have just given them permission to ignore you or discount your message, which, in spite of their finest intentions, they may do. Don't apologize.

Don't apologize for lack of skill. Instead, give them your absolute best. Show them you care about them by delivering your well-prepared message with enthusiasm and warmth. Developing your skill is far better than complaining about not having any.

Don't apologize for lack of knowledge. Instead, take the opportunity to deepen your knowledge seriously. There will always be those who have more knowledge than you. But that's not why you're speaking. You are speaking because of your particular insight and experience. That's something no one else can replicate. The Lord does not expect us to be experts in the gospel, He wants us to be experienced. "Be ye doers of the word, and not hearers only" (JAMES 1:22).

Don't apologize for lack of preparation. Instead, consecrate sufficient time to do it well. This is the least excusable. The US Postal Service has it right—"Neither rain, nor sleet, nor gloom of night . . . " It's easy to find excuses, but more satisfying to dedicate the time to do it right. Budget your time and stand before your ward members with a message that you know they need to hear.

Removing apologies from your speaking style is a significant change in attitude toward your assignment. Rejoice in the privilege and prepare to give your best.

Charge Up Your Battery

O that I were an angel, and could have the wish of mine heart, that I might go forth and speak with the trump of God, with a voice to shake the earth.

Alma 29:1

Deep in the lush jungles of Jamaica's Cockpit Country is a land riddled with limestone caves and underground rivers accessible only on foot. My husband and I, accompanied by two native guides, were given headlamps that would be the only source of light to illuminate the craggy and slippery floor of these extremely remote caves.

After an hour-long hike through the tropical forest, the vine-draped entrance of the cave and underground river appeared. Several times when stepping in water that appeared only ankle deep, I sank up to my knees or skidded over slippery rocks. We pushed deeper and deeper into this strange and isolated cave environment and further and further from the opening and any natural light.

Hours into our adventure, as I studied out the fascinating stalactite formations, I became aware that my headlamp was growing steadily dimmer. It never occurred to me that I might have to make my way back through those rivers without the benefit of light. The four of us were spread throughout the winding and intricate cave and I could hear the others' voices, but through the intense darkness and thick vapors—my first experience with "mists of darkness"—I could no longer see anyone in our party. How I ached for a little more light and a little more battery power.

In today's world, much of it ruled by the prince of darkness, we all yearn for light—light which comes from strong, fresh, powerful spirit-charged batteries.

From the pulpit, the audience wants to hear from speakers who are totally charged. Although sacrament meeting is a formal and reverent meeting, that does not mean that delivery should be tedious, dull, or soft-spoken. High-energy delivery is still compatible with a reverent style as you show your reverence for the gospel of Jesus Christ through your content, sources, vocabulary, dress, sincerity and testimony.

President Spencer W. Kimball counseled members to "[Speak] with enthusiasm and make them know you believe it."[1] Enthusiasm in your voice, facial expression and gestures communicate a passion for the topic and can simultaneously convey a spirit of reverence. The Savior has commanded, "Preach, exhort, declare the truth, even with a loud voice, with a sound of rejoicing, crying—Hosanna, hosanna, blessed be the name of the Lord God!" (D&C 19:37)

Note

1. *The Teachings of Spencer W. Kimball*, ed. Edward L. Kimball (1982), 517.

Full Text or Notes?

And thou shalt write upon the stones
all the words of this law very plainly.

Deuteronomy 27:8

My children love making rice pudding but have always been frustrated by my rather loose and ill-defined recipe. It has never been written down—just passed down.

Rice Pudding Recipe. Some rice, some water, some milk, some sugar and some cinnamon. Cook for a while. It will seem like forever. When it's done, eat it.

My children are particularly annoyed because they know I generally demand precision in recipe development. But for some reason, this recipe never seemed to require that sort of accuracy. We don't make it often, but when we do, the children hammer me with the same question—how much? They want exact amounts.

There are times when word-specific construction and delivery of a sermon is essential and other times when a more loosely defined style will work better. For some, a combination of the two works well. Learn the advantages and disadvantages of each style and you'll be prepared to use the method best-suited to your specific situation.

Manuscript Style

This is delivery from a complete full-text version of your sermon. Every word is pre-selected and crafted with care.

Advantages: You know exactly what word to say next, which gives a certain amount of confidence to the less-experienced speaker. Once rehearsed, you know precisely how long a sermon will take.

Disadvantages: It does take longer to write a full-text manuscript. You may find yourself inclined to read every word, which can cause delivery to become somewhat rigid and less expressive. Eye-contact may be diminished, which erodes the feeling of connection to your audience. You may need more than two or three pages if your talk is longer than eight minutes, which means more shuffling of paper at the pulpit.

Strategy to use successfully: Practice so thoroughly that your manuscript *disappears* and eye-contact is increased. Work at reading expressively so your message will come alive.

Extemporaneous Style

This is delivery from a well-crafted outline that has just enough information on it to keep you on-point each step of the way.

Advantages: You appear to be speaking spontaneously from the heart, almost as if the ideas are coming to you as you speak. It works best for topics you are well-versed in and comfortable speaking about. You should be able to give a 20-minute talk from a two-page outline.

Disadvantages: It takes serious rehearsal to be able to speak confidently and expressively from an outline. It can be unnerving to not remember a particular phrase. Timing can be a bit more unpredictable, but manageable if timing is noted in the margin.

Strategy to use successfully: Rehearse aloud numerous times, check timing with each rehearsal to be certain you are honoring the time limit given, and use colorful notations on your outline to keep you on-track. Have scripture passages ready to go.

Hybrid Style

This is a combination of the two—an outline for most of the sermon with some critical sections written out in full text. This will allow you to maximize eye contact and expressive delivery in the sections where you only need an outline while having the benefit of key passages written word for word.

Make Your Notes Work for You

And thus it is written. Amen.

Alma 6:8

If a dentist approached you with a dental instruction book and started reading how to drill on that tooth that's been bothering you, you might be understandably edgy. That does not mean that your dentist is lacking in competence. It just looks that way. The more people seem to know what they're doing, even if they're new at it, the more confidence we have in them.

The purpose of notes you bring to the pulpit is to remind you of the message that you have carefully prepared and rehearsed. Ward members want to hear from someone in whom they have confidence—someone who will enter into an inspiring gospel conversation with them, not someone who will timidly read the contents of a printed page to them.

Create a set of notes that are user-friendly and audience-friendly. Well-prepared notes allow you and your message to come alive. Here are some recommendations that will help you produce a set of speaker's notes that will work for you.

Paper. Use 8½″ x 11″ white paper, one side only. This keeps you from flipping pages during your talk. It also eliminates the possibility of getting confused as to where you are.

Try to limit your notes to 2–3 pages. The fewer pages you have, the less likely you'll lose your place. However, in a longer talk you may need more, especially if you are using a full-text manuscript. Be sure each page is numbered in the corner.

Text. Text printed from a computer is usually easier to read than handwritten text. Use a font large enough to read effortlessly. Double-space the text to make it easy to keep your place. If you can avoid taking reading glasses on and off while you speak, that will increase your eye contact with ward members. Practice speaking from your notes to confirm readability. If you choose to handwrite your talk, avoid torn-out spiral-bound pages or colored paper. Write clearly in waterproof black ink so you can use a highlighter. To conserve space, use standard outline format for sections you can do extemporaneously.

Wording. Use key words to remind you of each main point. Write out in full text any portions which you'll need to refer to or read (introduction, conclusion, extended quotes, poetry, etc.). If you are anxious about not finding the right page in the scriptures, write out the full text in your notes.

Scriptures. Mark your scriptures carefully so you know which passage you want to share. Discreetly placed sticky notes can be helpful. Use one to mark the page, with the reference written on the portion that sticks out. Use another to bracket the exact portion you want to quote.

Marking. To assist your delivery, you may want to mark main points with a highlighter, underline important words and use symbols for reminders. Design notes that work for you.

Presentation. You may find it helpful to place your notes in a folder or binder, taped in place or three-hole punched. This works better than folded pages which almost never can be fully flattened. When you stand to speak, set your notes on the pulpit and avoid shuffling or turning pages unnecessarily.

You can discreetly keep one hand on the page to mark where you are in the text.

Citations. If you quote from a general conference talk, be certain to have the citation with you in case someone asks. The same applies to any other books or articles quoted extensively. Always have the scripture references in your notes.

Rehearsal. Rehearse sufficiently to make notes seem to *disappear*. As you become more familiar with your text and need to look down less, listeners will feel you are talking *with* them rather than reading *to* them.

You now have a set of speaker's notes that are prepared to help you accomplish the sacred work you were called to do.

Eyes Are Upon You

The eyes of all Israel are upon thee.

1 Kings 1:20

The lifeguard at a public pool once explained that his job did not begin as he took his position up on the tower waiting to rescue a child in distress; it actually began as he entered the pool area. It was always the same routine. He walked in authoritatively with a whistle around his neck, greeted the children warmly, cleared the area of any dangers, and looked for any clusters of kids who seemed inclined to make trouble. He was making assessments, planning for the day and setting a tone of order and discipline. He knew that the children were watching and taking their cues from him. By deliberately preparing the opening moments of a day at the pool, the whole day seemed to go better.

Your speaking assignment may seem to be an isolated 20-minute segment in the middle of sacrament meeting, but you need to be aware that eyes are upon you from the moment you enter the chapel. For this one day, the ward will give you special attention. They'll take their cues from you and others on the stand. Will ward members draw the conclusion that this is a day of worship?

You may want to take a look at this list of recommended behaviors for those seated on the stand. They can contribute to a general feeling of reverence and help you feel more at ease. They are listed in the order you will most likely encounter in a typical sacrament meeting. Once on the stand, you are setting an example and preparing to speak, so only do those things conducive to the Spirit.

Before the Meeting

- ✦ Get a copy of the program and quietly check the arrangement of speakers.
- ✦ Avoid engaging in idle chatter.
- ✦ Smile and shake hands with other speakers and leaders on the stand.
- ✦ Take a seat where instructed by your priesthood leader.
- ✦ Determine the smoothest route to the pulpit, especially if you're seated on the second row.
- ✦ Be seated on the stand, fully prepared, five minutes before the meeting begins.
- ✦ Reverently listen to the prelude music.

During the Meeting

- ✦ Make certain you have a hymnal and sing each hymn.
- ✦ Listen to each speaker and special musical number.
- ✦ Sit up straight and be attentive throughout the meeting.
- ✦ Avoid turning to others on the stand or whispering during the meeting.
- ✦ Avoid crossing your legs, both for formality reasons and to make sure blood is circulating properly when you stand.
- ✦ Avoid working on your notes while on the stand; jotting down a phrase that helps you connect to those who speak before you is fine.
- ✦ Say "Amen" at the conclusion of each talk before or after you.

Getting Ready to Speak

- Have your scriptures out of their cover and your notes ready.
- Wait to stand until the previous speaker or the priesthood leader conducting is seated.
- Approach the podium with a brisk and dignified stride.
- Set your notes and scriptures gently on the podium.
- Adjust the microphone once.
- Pause briefly to make eye contact with the audience before beginning.
- Smile and begin.

After you have finished speaking, carefully gather your scriptures and notes and return to your seat. Remain on the stand until the meeting ends.

These simple steps will easily become routine over time. But if not considered in advance, you may find that you accidentally communicate a negative message before you begin. With just a little preparation, you can feel a deep inner peace knowing that you have contributed to the reverent tone of the meeting.

Shrink to Fit

Now the time is far passed.

Mark 6:35

While in college, I worked at a store which sold Levi jeans. My favorite ones to sell were the "100 percent cotton denim button-fly shrink-to-fit 501s". The trick in selling a pair of those jeans was helping customers imagine how well they would fit after the first washing. The idea was to buy them a little big in the waist and a couple of inches long in the length. Then, before wearing, wash the jeans in hot water. When you put them back on they would be snug, but eventually, the denim would adjust to the unique shape of your body. As a result, the fit was personal and comfortable.

That's the same feeling you want for your talk. But not every element of the "fit" can be managed in advance. Especially exasperating can be the moment of transition to the final talk in sacrament meeting.

When you're the last speaker, on occasion you may need to stretch or shrink your remarks to the remaining time. A glance at the clock can be somewhat unnerving. Although you were assigned 20 minutes, you may suddenly discover that the time slot has become three minutes . . . or 30 minutes. Flexibility, vision and warmth are the keys.

Flexibility. If you need to shorten your sermon, pull out the most important points and your finest example. If you need to fill an extra few minutes, pull out another story or example that underscores the importance of your topic. Learn in advance if you'll be the final speaker so you can have these strategies in place should they be needed.

Vision. Remember your mission statement. If you can keep your purpose in mind, then you will not be tempted to abandon the entire talk or to drift off in totally unrelated subjects. Keep your focus.

Warmth. If you have to shrink your talk, don't waste any time grousing that the ward has been robbed of hearing your full sermon. Jump right in with warmth and affection. The ward will respond with appreciation for your well-prepared remarks. If you need to stretch a bit, before standing make eye contact with the presiding priesthood authority, as he may want to use the remaining minutes to make final remarks. If it's left up to you, don't mention that you're scrambling to come up with something. Smile and begin with ultimate confidence. The Lord will bless you for being prepared.

Make Connections

The elements are eternal,
and spirit and element, inseparably connected,
receive a fulness of joy.

Doctrine and Covenants 93:33

Christmas is a season flooded with light—except when it comes to the Christmas tree. The dilemma is universal. Unless you get the connections just right between each string of lights, there is darkness instead of light. Without some attention, an entire side of the tree can be left in the shadows. With meticulous checking of each connector, suddenly there is light. Glorious, spine-tingling, sparkling light fills the room because every string is completely connected to the others.

To increase the feeling of light in sacrament meeting, connections also need to be made.

Connections give a feeling of wholeness. Connections should be pointed out by the speakers seamlessly and naturally. This allows the listeners to sense the associations of words, ideas, concepts and principles without making them struggle to dig them out while you're speaking. You have two options to accomplish this smoothly.

In advance. This first option is a little more stress-free, but requires a bit more homework. With just a couple of phone calls you should be able to find out who will be speaking or singing on the same program as you. A brief conversation with them is all it takes to gather scriptures, main points or lyrics. Discovering meaningful and powerful connections in the texts that will precede you will allow you to weave those ideas more strongly into your own text. Of course, that's not always possible.

On the stand. Your second option requires the ability to find common threads as ideas are delivered in sacrament meeting, in spoken or musical form. Rather than poring over your own notes, listen carefully to those who come before you. Whether the sacred ideas are being spoken or sung, phrases and concepts that relate to your message will stand out and can be built upon. But you have to be a little flexible. You'll be adding a phrase or two to your introduction. It may be helpful to jot something down in your notes.

As a result of this seemingly small effort:

- ✦ Your message will be more memorable.
- ✦ Messages preceding you will be more memorable.
- ✦ Musical phrases will fortify your message.
- ✦ Relationships will be strengthened.
- ✦ The overall theme of the meeting will be supported.

Remember, the connections you make need to be done gently. It takes surprisingly few words to achieve the desired effect. Showing respect and admiration for those who come before you increases the feeling of warmth and affection that should prevail among those who appear together in a sacrament meeting program. Connecting with those who precede you will make you and your message connect more fully with the audience.

Amen

Blessed be the Lord for evermore.
Amen, and Amen.

PSALM 89:52

Listen with the Spirit

Listen to the voice of him who speaketh.

Doctrine and Covenants 81:1

If you believe when you are invited to speak in sacrament meeting that the invitation was from the Lord, then you should apply the same belief system to everyone else who speaks. It's not just the Apostles at general conference; it's every speaker that ever addresses a congregation you're in. There's something important—perhaps even life changing—for you to hear and act upon. Knowing this should make you sit up and take notice.

You may find it worthwhile to begin taking notes in sacrament meeting. You don't need to produce a verbatim transcript of the proceedings, but you may want to jot down anything that stood out as applying to you right now. You can write in the program, on a piece of scratch paper or even in the margins of your scriptures. The act of writing it down multiplies the likelihood of remembering and taking action.

What is the speaker trying to tell me?
What is the main message I should remember?

Is there action I should take?
What is the Holy Spirit confirming in my heart?
When I say, "Amen," do I mean it?

Listening by the power of the Holy Spirit is every bit as essential to the process as speaking with that same power. And when you say, "Amen," it will resonate through your heart and through the generations.

Your Personal Testimony

This is the testimony, last of all, which we give of him:
That he lives!

Doctrine and Covenants 76:22

The phrase "famous last words" points out the improbability that before dying you will have the presence of mind or foresight to say something profound enough to be jotted down for posterity. In most cases, you don't know which ones are your last words.

But in the setting of a sermon in sacrament meeting, you can plan out your last words down to the final syllable. The closing words you speak have the potential to leave a remarkable and lasting impression. Although you want to project the feeling of a sincere and spontaneous testimony, you also want the impact of carefully selected words that will continue to resonate long after you've finished speaking. Write out those last few words and polish them until you can deliver them effortlessly. Check to see if these three elements are in your testimony.

1. Bear testimony of the principle or gospel topic you have spoken about.
2. Testify of the Savior's connection to your message.
3. Close in the name of Jesus Christ, Amen.

In his final general conference address, given just thirteen days before his death, Elder Bruce R. McConkie gave a testimony so potent and powerful it was almost tangible. Few who heard it will ever forget his emotion-filled witness of the Savior. "I testify that He is the Son of the Living God who was crucified for the sins of the world. He is our Lord, our God, and our King. This I know of myself independent of any other person. I am one of His Witnesses. And in the coming day I will feel the nail marks in His hands and in His feet and shall wet His feet with my tears. But I shall not know any better then than I know now that He is God's almighty Son and He is our Savior and Redeemer and that Salvation comes in and through His atoning blood and in no other way. . . . In the name of the Lord Jesus Christ, Amen."[1]

Note

1. "The Purifying Power of Gethsemane," *Ensign*, May 1985, 9.

Reverence for the Savior's Name

Bless the Lord, O my soul:
and all that is within me, bless his holy name.

Psalm 103:1

There are few hymns that strike a chord within the heart like "Jesus, the Very Thought of Thee." One of the oldest hymns in the LDS hymnal, the lyrics are attributed to Bernard of Clairvaux, a 12th-century monk in France whose devotion to the Savior and His teachings helped shape Christian theology of the era. In the face of hardships, deprivation and deteriorating health, Clairvaux's spirituality seemed to increase, leaving Christianity with treasured writings such as this hymn:

> Jesus, the very thought of thee with sweetness fills my breast.
> But sweeter far thy face to see and in thy presence rest.
> Nor voice can sing, nor heart can frame, nor can the memory find
> A sweeter sound than thy blest name, O Savior of mankind![1]

Singing that tender text elicits the deepest reverence for the Savior, making it possible to find solace in the sound of His name alone. Yet simply knowing the power and majesty of invoking the Savior's name, is not always enough to generate the solemnity that is due at the close of a sermon. The final words from a speaker's mouth complete the message in the minds of the listener, placing the Savior's name as a sacred seal.

Here are a few items to consider that will help you to prepare to elevate the reverent tone of those last few moments at the pulpit:

- ✦ **Work toward having a testimony** that what you have said is true and is what the Lord would have you say; you will feel more confident about closing in His name.
- ✦ **Close in the name of Jesus Christ**, a name and title, not just "Jesus," as that is a name shared by others besides the Savior.
- ✦ **Avoid saying "in the name of *thy* son,"** as you might in a prayer, as you are addressing ward members, not the Father.
- ✦ **Honor the name of the Savior** by slowing down and deliberately stating His name clearly as the seal on your testimony.
- ✦ **Look up as you say your final words**—you certainly have no need to read them. Your eye contact with ward members will increase the feeling of sincerity.
- ✦ **Your last words are not to be rushed through** as if by saying them you are granted exit from an uncomfortable place. Speak them as if you are showing ultimate respect for the privilege of speaking in the name of Christ.
- ✦ **Allow the ward to respond** with their "Amen" before you leave the podium and return reverently to your seat.

Note

1. "Jesus, the Very Thought of Thee," *Hymns*, no. 141.

Amen

Now the God of peace be with you all. Amen.

Romans 15:33

What does the word "Amen" mean? More importantly, what does it mean to you?

It's possible that some believe "Amen" means "I'm finished talking" or even "I'm going to sit down now." Based on how casually it is sometimes used, that could be what the word has come to mean. A little refresher course on this tiny word may be in order.

The word "Amen" comes from a Hebrew verb *aman* meaning to strengthen or confirm and was accepted by the early Christian Church because the word was used by the Savior so frequently.

Within the Church today "Amen" is used as a word of acceptance of truth (at the close of a talk or testimony), shared affirmation (at the conclusion of a prayer or blessing) or the acceptance of a covenant (baptism). In each circumstance, "Amen" is a method declaring to the Lord and others your response to someone else's words.

President Spencer W. Kimball was especially adamant about our responsibility to respond with an enthusiastic "Amen" at the conclusion of a sermon. "Will you always say 'Amen'? Never fail. That means 'so be it, what has been said is agreeable to me.'"[1] He later counseled, "Every time that a sermon is concluded . . . every man, woman, and child should say 'Amen,' loud enough so that the person next to him or her can hear it."[2]

Amen is an invitation by the speaker to respond to the truths discussed. The tradition of closing a talk with "Amen" hints at the responsibility the speaker has to declare eternal truth with clarity and power. Members of the congregation then have the responsibility to reply in full voice, "Amen."

May every sermon you deliver be worthy of a resounding "Amen."

Notes

1. *The Teachings of Spencer W. Kimball,* ed. Edward L. Kimball (1982), 522–23.
2. Ibid., 520.

Worksheet

Sermon Preparation Outline

Sacrament Meeting Sermon Preparation Outline

This worksheet is designed to help you work through all the components of a well-organized and well-researched sacrament meeting sermon. Prayerfully consider each part until the process becomes second nature.

Date to Speak:

Priesthood Contact:

Theme to Meeting:

Position in Meeting (beginning, middle, end):

Assigned Length:

Remember, you will normally speak 120–150 words per minute. You'll need to set aside about one hour of preparation time for each one minute you are assigned to speak.

Topic:

Prayerfully select and make sure you have it sufficiently narrowed.

Consider the Congregation:

Write down how ward members feel about the topic and what they generally know. Consider the demographics of the ward. Keep them in mind as you create your message.

Mission:

Write down what you want ward members top know, do, feel or believe as a result of your sermon. Choose your focus—Inspire, Motivate or Explain. Draft a mission statement using one of those words.

Inspire (Help ward members feel positive about a gospel topic)
Motivate (Encourage ward members to take a specific course of action)
Explain (Assist ward members to understand a principle more deeply or accurately)

Scriptural Foundation:

Research what prophets, ancient and modern, have said about this topic. Select a specific scripture passage or quote from a prophet that becomes your foundation.

Message:

Write down the message you want ward members to remember when you are finished speaking.

Main Points:

Consider the most effective way to organize main points to accomplish your stated mission. Limit yourself to 2 to 5 main points with sub-points as needed. Use a variety of support including testimony, scriptures, quotes from general conference talks, hymns, examples, stories, parables, personal experiences, statistics, etc.

1.

2.

3.

Introduction:

1) Connect; 2) Attract; 3) Reveal; 4) Establish; 5) Map

Conclusion:

1) Signal; 2) Reinforce; 3) Restate; 4) Close; 5) Seal

Testimony:

Be certain to bear testimony of the principle you are speaking about.

Note: This is a worksheet to get you thinking and brainstorming. Now take these pieces and arrange them into a sermon.

This worksheet is available to download for free at www.perihelionpress.com